The Making of
THE AMERICAN
PARTY SYSTEM
1789 to 1809

Edited by
Noble E. Cunningham, Jr.

PRENTICE-HALL, INC.
Englewood Cliffs, N. J.

In Memory of
CHARLES S. SYDNOR

Current printing (last digit):

11   10   9   8   7   6   5   4   3   2

CONTENTS

III. THE PARTY MANAGERS   65

VI. THE NATIONAL NOMINATING CAUCUS 123

The Making of

THE AMERICAN
PARTY SYSTEM
1789 to 1809

INTRODUCTION

"A politician in this country must be the man of a party," wrote John Quincy Adams in his diary in 1802. "I would fain be the man of my whole country." Adams's observation reflected both the common realization that parties had become an essential part of the American political system and the general reluctance to view parties as being in the national interest. A decade earlier, no American would have suggested that party affiliation was necessary for political success, and those who mentioned parties did so only with words of admonition. Now, only five years after George Washington had left the presidency, though admonitions still continued, parties were a recognized part of the working political structure.

The Federalist and Anti-Federalist divisions over the ratification of the Constitution had not continued in the new government that began operation in 1789. The Constitution had not anticipated political parties and, in fact, had been constructed with the hope of discouraging factions. President Washington regarded himself as being above parties and attempted to reconcile all groups to his administration. When his Cabinet became divided by the differences between Secretary of State Thomas Jefferson and Secretary of the Treasury Alexander Hamilton, he diligently tried to heal the breach. In his final political testament, a farewell address to the nation, he warned against the dangers of parties. Yet by the time Washington left office in 1797, the Republican and the Federalist parties had become fairly clearly defined. The election of 1796 was the nation's first party contest for the presidency, from which the Federalist candidate John Adams emerged victorious by a margin of three electoral votes over his Republican opponent Thomas Jefferson.

Neither the Federalist party nor the Republican party had sprung suddenly into being, and neither was solely the result of the contest between Hamilton and Jefferson. The differences between these two members of Washington's Cabinet had an important part in the emergence of parties, but of even greater importance in the actual formation of parties was the gradual growth of two opposing factions in Congress which provided the nuclei of the Federalist and the Republican parties. In the House of Representatives, James Madison became the chief leader of the opposition to Hamilton and played a major role in the formation of the Republican party. During the years of Jefferson's retirement from public life from 1793 to 1797, Madison carried the principal burden of party leadership, and Congress was the center from which party divisions spread throughout the nation.

The election of John Adams as President and of a Federalist majority in Congress in 1796 brought the first distinct party administration of the national government, and the Federalist management of the government created the principal party issues to be contested in Adams's bid for re-election. As runner-up in the election of 1796, Jefferson served, under the system which prevailed until the adoption of the Twelfth Amendment in 1804, as Vice-President under Adams, but he was clearly not a part of the administration, and he assumed command of the Republican party and mobilized it for the party battle of 1800. Jefferson's leadership was accompanied by extensive Republican party organizational efforts in a number of states in preparation for the election of 1800. This hard-fought election was in every sense a contest of parties.

Jefferson's victory over Adams and the election of a Republican Congress brought in 1801 the first transfer of political power in the national government from one political party to another. The Republican party was then faced with the responsibilities of power, the problems created by the party change-over, and the task of staying in office. The re-election of Jefferson in 1804 and the election of Madison as his successor in 1808 demonstrated that the Republican party had survived the test of power. Thus, within the span of three presidential administrations, the American party system had been established and proved workable, and with it had been formed many of the patterns of political conduct that were to become familiar features of political life in the United States.

The documents in this book have been selected to illustrate the formation and operation of national political parties during the first two decades under the Constitution. Embracing the presidential administrations of Washington, Adams, and Jefferson, they display the emergence of parties during Washington's presidency, their growing maturity during Adams's administration, and the perfecting of party mechanisms and techniques under President Jefferson. The documents reveal the contemporary misgivings about political parties, the broad principles and specific issues which provided the rationale for participation in the party contest, and the practical operation of parties as political institutions: party management and machinery, campaign practices, and partisan uses of the press and of patronage. Through the contemporary records, the development of parties can be seen realistically in the debates over practical issues, in party efforts to marshal public support, and in party problems of nominating candidates, getting nominees elected to office, preserving party unity, and staying in power once office was obtained. Although most participants were too involved in the problems of their own day to appreciate the broad significance of the development of responsible parties, the device of party, the record shows, served the process by which the aspirations of the electorate were translated into political action.

Not everything that early Americans did in forming and operating parties can be reconstructed from the documents, for there were some cautious party managers who rarely committed any of their plans to paper. But the slowness of transportation and communication made it necessary that many party plans be worked out through private correspondence and by means of printed party communications, and these documents offer revealing insights into the making of the American party system.

The Jeffersonians generally referred to themselves as Republicans, though in a few places the names *Democrat* and *Democratic Republican* came to be used. By their opponents they were frequently called anti-Federalists, Jacobins, and disorganizers. On the other hand, Republicans often referred to the Federalists as anti-Republicans, monarchists, and Tories. Since *Republican* and *Federalist* were the names most generally used in self-designation, they have been used in the editorial notes.

Due to the nature of the contemporary sources, and in order to embrace as broad an area as possible while providing some probing in depth, the entire period from 1789 to 1809 has not been covered in each chapter. Thus, Chapter II concentrates on the period before 1801, when party conflict brought issues and ideologies most sharply into view; Chapter VI focuses on the congressional nominating caucuses of 1804 and 1808 because these are the best documented; and Chapter IX is restricted to party patronage under Jefferson because of the new circumstances occasioned by the Republican assumption of power in 1801.

Only primary sources have been included in these selections, and introductory notes and headings serve essentially to place the documents in historical perspective. Except where modification seems necessary for clarity, archaic and erratic spelling and punctuation have been retained in order to preserve as far as possible the style and flavor of the original documents. It is hoped that the student of political parties and of early national history will find profitable the opportunity to explore firsthand the origins and the workings of the early party system in the United States.

I THE CONCEPT OF POLITICAL PARTIES IN THE EARLY REPUBLIC

Those Americans who laid the foundations for the successful party system of the United States had no intention of constructing a party system as a permanent part of the American political structure. The most striking attitude that permeated whatever was said or done in relation to early party formation was the idea that parties were evils to be avoided or, failing in that, devices whose dangerous tendencies were to be checked. Most of the thought given to the subject of parties reflected this negative approach. The framers of the Constitution clearly did not anticipate the party system, and even those who participated in the formation of parties rarely attempted to justify their actions in terms of a party system. Many contemporaries saw the early party struggle through which they lived in the simple terms with which so sophisticated a theorist as Thomas Jefferson once equated it: "the parties of Honest men, and Rogues, into which every country is divided." Although Jefferson wrote that "in every free and deliberating society there must, from the nature of man, be opposite parties" and suggested that "perhaps this party division is necessary," it is clear from Jefferson's actions that he did not think in terms of a permanent party system. He himself never admitted the validity of the Federalist party, and he began his presidency following the party victory of 1800 with serious, though unsuccessful, efforts to reconcile parties and unite the electorate. Jefferson's affirmation in his inaugural address that "we are all republicans—we are all federalists" was no idle gesture.

Lacking a theoretical basis, American parties evolved from pragmatic experience.

1 "THE VIOLENCE OF FACTION"

In *The Federalist*, Number 10, James Madison clearly demonstrates that the authors of the Constitution did not conceive of political parties as responsible elements of representative government. Making no distinction in his essay between *faction* and *party*, Madison defined his concept of faction and examined its basis, placing particular emphasis on economic factors. Jacob E. Cooke, ed., *The Federalist* (Middletown, Conn.: 1961), 56-65.

Among the numerous advantages promised by a well constructed Union, none deserves to be more accurately developed than its tendency to break and control the violence of faction. The friend of popular governments, never finds himself so much alarmed for their character and fate, as when he contemplates their propensity to this dangerous vice. He will not fail therefore to set a due value on any plan which, without violating the principles to which he is attached, provides a proper cure for it. . . .

By a faction I understand a number of citizens, whether amounting to a majority or minority of the whole, who are united and actuated by some common impulse of passion, or of interest, adverse to the rights of other citizens, or to the permanent and aggregate interests of the community.

There are two methods of curing the mischiefs of faction: the one, by removing its causes; the other, by controling its effects.

There are again two methods of removing the causes of faction: the one by destroying the liberty which is essential to its existence; the other, by giving to every citizen the same opinions, the same passions, and the same interests.

It could never be more truly said than of the first remedy, that it is worse than the disease. Liberty is to faction, what air is to fire, an aliment without which it instantly expires. But it could not be a less folly to abolish liberty, which is essential to political life, because it nourishes faction, than it would be to wish the annihilation of air, which is essential to animal life, because it imparts to fire its destructive agency.

The second expedient is as impracticable, as the first would be unwise. As long as the reason of man continues fallible, and he is at liberty to exercise it, different opinions will be formed. As long as the connection subsists between his reason and his self-love, his opinions and his passions will have a reciprocal influence on each other; and the former will be objects to which the latter will attach themselves. The diversity in the faculties of men from which the rights of property originate, is not less an insuperable obstacle to a uniformity of interests. The protection of these faculties is the first object of Government. From the protection of different and unequal faculties of acquiring property, the possession of different degrees and kinds of property immediately results: and from the influence of these on the sentiments and views of the respective proprietors, ensues a division of the society into different interests and parties.

The latent causes of faction are thus sown in the nature of man; and we see them every where brought into different degrees of activity, according to the different circumstances of civil society. A zeal for different opinions concerning religion, concerning Government and many other points, as well of speculation as of practice; an attachment to different leaders ambitiously contending for pre-eminence and power; or to persons of other descriptions whose fortunes have been interesting to the human passions, have in turn divided mankind into parties, inflamed them with mutual animosity, and rendered them much more disposed to vex and oppress each other, than to co-operate for their common good. So strong is this propensity of mankind to fall into mutual animosities, that where no substantial occasion presents itself, the most frivolous and fanciful distinctions have been sufficient to kindle their unfriendly passions, and excite their most violent conflicts. But the most common and durable source of factions, has been the various and unequal distribution of property. Those who hold, and those who are without property, have ever formed distinct interests in society. Those who are creditors, and those who are debtors, fall under a like discrimination. A landed interest, a manufacturing interest, a mercantile interest, a monied interest, with many lesser interests, grow up of necessity in civilized nations, and divide them into different classes, actuated by different sentiments and views. The regulation of these various and interfering interests forms the principal task of modern Legislation, and involves the spirit of party and faction in the necessary and ordinary operations of Government. . . .

It is in vain to say, that enlightened statesmen will be able to adjust these clashing interests, and render them all subservient to the public good. Enlightened statesmen will not always be at the helm: Nor, in many cases, can such an adjustment be made at all, without taking into view indirect and remote considerations, which will rarely prevail over the immediate interest which one party may find in disregarding the rights of another, or the good of the whole.

The inference to which we are brought, is, that the *causes* of faction cannot be removed; and that relief is only to be sought in the means of controling its *effects*.

If a faction consists of less than a majority, relief is supplied by the republican principle, which enables the majority to defeat its sinister views by regular vote: It may clog the administration, it may convulse the society; but it will be unable to execute and mask its violence under the forms of the Constitution. When a majority is included in a faction, the form of popular government on the other hand enables it to sacrifice to its ruling passion or interest, both the public good and the rights of other citizens. To secure the public good, and private rights, against the danger of such a faction, and at the same time to preserve the spirit and the form of popular government, is then the great object to which our enquiries are directed: Let me add that it is the great desideratum, by which alone this form of government can be rescued from the opprobrium under which it has so long labored, and be recommended to the esteem and adoption of mankind.

By what means is this object attainable? Evidently by one of two only. Either the existence of the same passion or interest in a majority at the same time, must be prevented; or the majority, having such co-existent passion or interest, must be rendered, by their number and local situation, unable to concert and carry into effect schemes of oppression. If the impulse and the opportunity be suffered to coincide, we well know that neither moral nor religious motives can be relied on as adequate control. They are not found to be such on the injustice and violence of individuals, and lose their efficacy in proportion to the number combined together; that is, in proportion as their efficacy becomes needful.

From this view of the subject, it may be concluded, that a pure Democracy, by which I mean, a Society, consisting of a small number of citizens, who assemble and administer the Government in person, can admit of no cure for the mischiefs of faction. A common passion or interest will, in almost every case, be felt by a majority of the whole; a communication and concert results from the form of Government itself; and there is nothing to check the inducements to sacrifice the weaker party, or an obnoxious individual. Hence it is, that such Democracies have ever been spectacles of turbulence and contention; have ever been found incompatible with personal security, or the rights of property; and have in general been as short in their lives, as they have been violent in their deaths. Theoretic politicians, who have patronized this species of Government, have erroneously supposed, that by reducing mankind to a perfect equality in their political rights, they would, at the same time, be perfectly equalized and assimilated in their possessions, their opinions, and their passions.

A Republic, by which I mean a Government in which the scheme of representation takes place, opens a different prospect, and promises the cure for which we are seeking. Let us examine the points in which it varies from pure Democracy, and we shall comprehend both the nature of the cure, and the efficacy which it must derive from the Union.

The two great points of difference between a Democracy and a Republic are, first, the delegation of the Government, in the latter, to a small number of citizens elected by the rest: secondly, the greater number of citizens, and greater sphere of country, over which the latter may be extended. . . .

. . . The smaller the society, the fewer probably will be the distinct parties and interests composing it; the fewer the distinct parties and interests, the more frequently will a majority be found of the same party; and the smaller the number of individuals composing a majority, and the smaller the compass within which they are placed, the more easily will they concert and execute their plans of oppression. Extend the sphere, and you take in a greater variety of parties and interests; you make it less probable that a majority of the whole will have a common motive to invade the rights of other citizens; or if such a common motive exists, it will be more difficult for all who feel it to discover their own strength, and to act in unison with each other. Besides other impediments, it may be remarked, that where there is a consciousness of unjust or dishonorable purposes, communication is always checked by distrust, in proportion to the number whose concurrence is necessary.

Hence it clearly appears, that the same advantage, which a Republic has over a Democracy, in controling the effects of faction, is enjoyed by a large over a small Republic—is enjoyed by the Union over the States composing it. Does this advantage consist in the substitution of Representatives, whose enlightened views and virtuous sentiments render them superior to local prejudices, and to schemes of injustice? It will not be denied, that the Representation of the Union will be most likely to possess these requisite endowments. Does it consist in the greater security afforded by a greater variety of parties, against the event of any one party being able to outnumber and oppress the rest? In an equal degree does the encreased variety of parties, comprised within the Union, encrease this security. Does it, in fine, consist in the greater obstacles opposed to the concert and accomplishment of the secret wishes of an unjust and interested majority? Here, again, the extent of the Union gives it the most palpable advantage.

The influence of factious leaders may kindle a flame within their particular States, but will be unable to spread a general conflagration through the other States: a religious sect, may degenerate into a political faction in a part of the Confederacy; but the variety of sects dispersed over the entire face of it, must secure the national Councils against any danger from that source: a rage for paper money, for an abolition of debts, for an equal division of property, or for any other improper or wicked project, will be less apt to pervade the whole body of the Union, than a particular member of it; in the same proportion as such a malady is more likely to taint a particular county or district, than an entire State.

In the extent and proper structure of the Union, therefore, we behold a Republican remedy for the diseases most incident to Republican Government. And according to the degree of pleasure and pride, we feel in being Republicans, ought to be our zeal in cherishing the spirit, and supporting the character of Federalists.

2 "A CANDID STATE OF PARTIES"

Writing for the Philadelphia *National Gazette*, September 26, 1792, Madison offered a brief interpretation of earlier political divisions in the United States and described, as he saw them, the party divisions in 1792. Gaillard Hunt, ed., *The Writings of James Madison* (New York: 1900-1910), VI, 106-19.

As it is the business of the contemplative statesman to trace the history of parties in a free country, so it is the duty of the citizen at all times to understand the actual state of them. Whenever this duty is omitted, an opportunity is given to designing men, by the use of artificial or nominal distinctions, to oppose and balance against each other those who never differed as to the end to be pursued, and may no longer differ as to the means of attaining it. The most interesting state of parties in the United States may be referred to three periods: Those who espoused the cause of independence and those who adhered to the British claims, formed the parties of the first period; if, indeed, the disaffected class were considerable enough to deserve the name of a party. This state of things was superseded by the treaty of peace in 1783. From 1783 to 1787 there were parties in abundance, but being rather local than general, they are not within the present review.

The Federal Constitution, proposed in the latter year, gave birth to a second and most interesting division of the people. Every one remembers it, because every one was involved in it.

Among those who embraced the constitution, the great body were unquestionably friends to republican liberty; tho' there were, no doubt, some who were openly or secretly attached to monarchy and aristocracy; and hoped to make the constitution a cradle for these hereditary establishments.

Among those who opposed the constitution, the great body were certainly well affected to the union and to good government, tho' there might be a few who had a leaning unfavourable to both. This state of parties was terminated by the regular and effectual establishment of the federal government in 1788; out of the administration of which, however, has arisen a third division, which being natural to most political societies, is likely to be of some duration in ours.

One of the divisions consists of those, who from particular interest, from natural temper, or from the habits of life, are more partial to the opulent than to the other classes of society; and having debauched themselves into a persuasion that mankind are incapable of governing themselves, it follows with them, of course, that government can be carried on only by the pageantry of rank, the influence of money and emoluments, and the terror of military force. Men of those sentiments must naturally wish to point the measures of government less to the interest of the many than of a few, and less to the reason of the many than to their weaknesses; hoping perhaps in proportion to the ardor of their zeal, that by giving such a turn to the administration, the government itself may by degrees be narrowed into fewer hands, and approximated to an hereditary form.

The other division consists of those who believing in the doctrine that mankind are capable of governing themselves, and hating hereditary power as an insult to the reason and an outrage to the rights of man, are naturally offended at every public measure that does not appeal to the understanding and to the general interest of the community, or that is not strictly conformable to the principles, and conducive to the preservation of republican government.

This being the real state of parties among us, an experienced and dispassionate observer will be at no loss to decide on the probable conduct of each.

The anti republican party, as it may be called, being the weaker in point of numbers, will be induced by the most obvious motives to strengthen themselves with the men of influence, particularly of moneyed, which is the most active and insinuating influence. It will be equally their true policy to weaken their opponents by reviving exploded parties, and taking advantage of all prejudices, local, political, and occupational, that may prevent or disturb a general coalition of sentiments.

The republican party, as it may be termed, conscious that the mass of people in every part of the union, in every state, and of every occupation must at bottom be with them, both in interest and sentiments, will naturally find their account in burying all antecedent questions, in banishing every other distinction than that between enemies and friends to republican government, and in promoting a general harmony among the latter, wherever residing, or however employed. . . .

3 "PARTY SPIRIT"

William Wyche, a New York jurist, expounded on the evils of parties in an address to the Horanian Literary Society, May 10, 1794. Wyche, *Party Spirit* (New York: 1794), 10-19, New York Public Library.

The independence of this country, obtained by the just efforts of an enlightened people, has procured it happiness and ease. Far opposite to the views and wishes of a disappointed few, the government has been happily organized; its wheels have smoothly ran, and prosperity has blessed the United States. A scene of harmony and order is displayed, and the flourishing state of the country evinces the progress of liberty. The divisions which existed during the war have, however, given rise to a factious spirit, which frequently disturbs the peace of America. The dissentions which then prevailed, the difference of sentiment hence originating in the minds of men, together with the variety of characters constantly emigrating, have naturally created a difference of opinion. We may view this pernicious spirit of party, Proteus like, in a thousand different shapes: uniform, indeed, in one point —the production of hatred and animosity. At one time we hear of *Whigs* and *Tories;* at another of *Clintonians* and *Jayites;* now of *Aristocrats* and *Democrats.* Let party assume what name it will, it is at all times attended with the same ill consequences.

A distinction of this nature is inconsistent with true freedom. Liberty ought to have no enemies; she proclaims the happiness of man; her foe is then the foe of man, and deserves to be hunted as a beast of prey. The being who willingly submits himself to the despotic rule of one, in losing the privileges of his nature, descends from the rank of humanity. He must be either ignorant or meanly interested. In the first case, I pity his situation; in the latter, I treat him with contempt: actuated by views of interest, he deserves the greatest punishment man can inflict. The title of *aristocrat,* justly bestowed, conveys the idea of all that is despicable in man. I cannot, however, entertain so ill an opinion of my fellow creatures as to suppose any here are now under the influence of despotism. Faction must now rise from a different source; all alike feel the same desire in support of their liberties, but they differ in the means. A uniform principle, I hope, directs the conduct of all, but they divide in its pursuit. The opposition and party spirit observable in this country, arise in many from the blindness of their zeal. Animated in the cause of freedom, they mistake the shadow for the substance, and employ themselves in catching at its empty traces on the wall, while the body itself glides away. The very name of republicanism inspires some mad enthusiasts, but they only view her with a jaundiced eye. The vain motive of appearing in the public prints as advocates for liberty, creates a number of pretended patriots, who would never have signalized themselves, if they did not expect fame and honors to attend their steps. Zealous themselves they cannot bear moderation in others, and hence treat it with contemptuous scorn. This is the origin of deadly hatred; the latter cannot brook what they cannot conceive they merited; and an opposition ensues which may possibly involve the peace of America. For my part, I feel an utter aversion to regal power; and, I trust, I shall ever deserve the name of a zealous advocate for that liberty, which is the dearest right of man; but, I must confess, I do not see a necessity for bespattering the character of a man, who differs from me in opinion. I will hear him candidly and coolly, and, while I deny assent to his doctrines, will treat him as a fellow creature. The idle distinctions of *aristocrat* and *democrat* I would bury in oblivion, and treat none as enemies but those who would deprive me of my liberty.

In examining the history of nations, we discover examples of the pernicious tendency of faction. In the mortal conflict which existed between the houses of York and Lancaster, related in the English annals, we sufficiently see its dreadful effects. Long and bloody were the wars which it produced, and horrible to behold was the animosity which then prevailed. The sword of the father was lifted over the head of the son, and the arrow of the child struck at the heart of his parent. Thousands were massacred for a difference in opinion, and the whole land was a deluge of blood. The peaceable instruments of agriculture were converted into weapons of war, and merciless faction, with fire and sword, penetrated into the bowels of Britain. Civil commotions oppressed the people, and the unfortunate widow and orphan became the dreadful victims of popular fury. The dire ravages of faction thus experienced were long felt in this nation; a considerable period elapsed before she re-assumed her former vigor. The little commerce she had was at a stop; her riches were exhausted; and she wanted nothing but an attack to render her the prey of foreign despots.

View the situation of France when torn with the disputes between the Catholics and Huguenots. Behold the sacrifice of thousands for holding those religious tenets they conceived consistent with reason. The man, who exercised this rational liberty of thinking for himself, was exorcised by the prevailing party of the times, and exterminated from the earth by the most cruel torturing death that bigotry could devise, or superstitious rage could execute—by burning in a slow and lingering flame.

To take an example more immediately analogous to America, let us recur to ancient periods, and inquire what caused the fall of Athens? Faction: the spirit of discord prevailed, and liberty was destroyed. A few popular characters, by the force of eloquence alone, were able to lead the multitude. Each great man had his party; the disputes of the leaders were supported by their followers, and peace fled from the government. An Aeschines and a Demosthenes mutually accused each other of corruption, and the whole time of the state was employed in determining their recriminations. The consequences at last proved fatal, and the Macedonian tyrant soon gained an easy conquest. Party feuds shook the republic to her centre, and delivered her to the conqueror.

The republic of Rome experienced a similar fate. Ambitious Caesar saw the moment when party blinded the vigilance of his country's friends, seized it, and triumphed. In this instance he might truly have said, He came—he saw—he conquered.

This fatal shore, on which so many nations have been stranded, is destined to produce the same fate to America, unless the spirit of party be repressed. The inevitable destruction arising from disunion must, in all situations, have a uniform tendency. To divide and conquer has been the universal maxim of insidious ministers, whose objects were to carry measures dangerous to the common weal: it is, indeed, a maxim extremely well calculated to answer this end, for those who are vigilant in defence of their party are dormant in that of their country. Party is a monster who devours the common good, whose destructive jaws are dangerous to the felicity of nations. . . .

Party has been a subject of declamation and discussion for ages; but it still exists; the efforts of men have not been able to root it up. The period will arrive, we may yet hope, when her destructive influence will cease, and when we may view a restoration of harmony. The arts of faction must decrease in an enlightened age; the rising progress of civilization must overpower her dominion, and produce peace and happiness to future generations. . . .

4 "THE DANGER OF PARTIES"

The most famous contemporary warning against the danger of parties came from President Washington in his Farewell Address, September 19, 1796. Washington, who considered himself above parties, had been disturbed by the divisions within his administration and by the spread of parties throughout the Union. Although Washington's motives may be considered nonpartisan, it is reasonable to assume that Alexander Hamilton, who assisted the President in the writing of his address, had the Republicans in mind in the denunciation of parties. John C. Fitzpatrick, ed., *The Writings of George Washington* (Washington: 1931-44), XXXV, 223-28.

In contemplating the causes which may disturb our Union, it occurs as matter of serious concern, that any ground should have been furnished for characterizing parties by *Geographical* discriminations: *Northern* and *Southern; Atlantic* and *Western;* whence designing men may endeavour to excite a belief that there is a real difference of local interests and views. One of the expedients of Party to acquire influence, within particular districts, is to misrepresent the opinions and aims of other Districts. You cannot shield yourselves too much against the jealousies and heart burnings which spring from these misrepresentations. They tend to render Alien to each other those who ought to be bound together by fraternal affection. . . .

To the efficacy and permanency of Your Union, a Government for the whole is indispensable. No Alliances however strict between the parts can be an adequate substitute. They must inevitably experience the infractions and interruptions which all Alliances in all times have experienced. Sensible of this momentous truth, you have improved upon your first essay, by the adoption of a Constitution of Government, better calculated than your former for an intimate Union, and for the efficacious management of your common concerns. This government, the offspring of our own choice uninfluenced and unawed, adopted upon full investigation and mature deliberation, completely free in its principles, in the distribution of its powers, uniting security with energy, and containing within itself a provision for its own amendment, has a just claim to your confidence and your support. Respect for its authority, compliance with its Laws, acquiescence in its measures, are duties enjoined by the fundamental maxims of true Liberty. The basis of our political systems is the right of the people to make and to alter their Constitutions of Government. But the Constitution which at any time exists, 'till changed by an explicit and authentic act of the whole People, is sacredly obligatory upon all. The very idea of the power and the right of the People to establish Government presupposes the duty of every Individual to obey the established Government.

All obstructions to the execution of the Laws, all combinations and Associations, under whatever plausible character, with the real design to direct, controul, counteract, or awe the regular deliberation and action of the Constituted authorities are distructive of this fundamental principle and of fatal tendency. They serve to organize faction, to give it an artificial and extraordinary force; to put in the place of the delegated will of the Nation, the will of a party; often a small but artful and enterprizing minority of the Community; and, according to the alternate triumphs of different parties, to make the public administration the Mirror of the ill concerted and incongruous projects of faction, rather than the organ of consistent and wholesome plans digested by common councils and modified by mutual interests. However combinations or Associations of the above description may now and then answer popular ends, they are likely, in the course of time and things, to become potent engines, by which cunning, ambitious and unprincipled men will be enabled to subvert the Power of the People, and to usurp for themselves the reins of Government; destroying afterwards the very engines which have lifted them to unjust dominion. . . .

I have already intimated to you the danger of Parties in the State, with particular reference to the founding of them on Geographical discriminations. Let me now take a more comprehensive view, and warn you in the most solemn manner against the baneful effects of the Spirit of Party, generally.

This spirit, unfortunately, is inseperable from our nature, having its root in the strongest passions of the human Mind. It exists under different shapes in all Governments, more or less stifled, controuled, or repressed; but, in those of the popular form it is seen in its greatest rankness and is truly their worst enemy.

The alternate domination of one faction over another, sharpened by the spirit of revenge natural to party dissention, which in different ages and countries has perpetrated the most horrid enormities, is itself a frightful despotism. But this leads at length to a more formal and permanent despotism. The disorders and miseries, which result, gradually incline the minds of men to seek security and repose in the absolute power of an Individual: and sooner or later the chief of some prevailing faction more able or more fortunate than his competitors, turns this disposition to the purposes of his own elevation, on the ruins of Public Liberty.

Without looking forward to an extremity of this kind (which nevertheless ought not to be entirely out of sight) the common and continual mischiefs of the spirit of Party are sufficient to make it the interest and the duty of a wise People to discourage and restrain it.

It serves always to distract the Public Councils and enfeeble the Public administration. It agitates the Community with ill founded jealousies and false alarms, kindles the animosity of one part against another, foments occasionally riot and insurrection. It opens the door to foreign influence and corruption, which find a facilitated access to the government itself through the channels of party passions. Thus the policy and the will of one country, are subjected to the policy and will of another.

There is an opinion that parties in free countries are useful checks upon the Administration of the Government and serve to keep alive the spirit of Liberty. This within certain limits is probably true, and in Governments of a Monarchical cast Patriotism may look with endulgence, if not with favour, upon the spirit of party. But in those of the popular character, in Governments purely elective, it is a spirit not to be encouraged. From their natural tendency, it is certain there will always be enough of that spirit for every salutary purpose. And there being constant danger of excess, the effort ought to be, by force of public opinion, to mitigate and assuage it. A fire not to be quenched; it demands a uniform vigilance to prevent its bursting into a flame, lest instead of warming it should consume.

5 THOMAS JEFFERSON ON PARTIES

Viewing party divisions as natural to political society, Jefferson emphasized differing principles as the explanation and justification for party divisions in the United States. He recognized the usefulness of party devices to achieve political success, and he adeptly employed them to that end, yet he never seems to have thought in terms of an institutionalized party system as a permanent part of the nation's political structure. Paul L. Ford, ed., *The Writings of Thomas Jefferson* (New York: 1892-99), VII, 43; Massachusetts Historical Society, *Collections*, Ser. 7, I (1900), 61-64; *American Historical Review*, III (1898), 488-89; Jefferson Papers, Library of Congress; Lester J. Cappon, ed., *The Adams-Jefferson Letters* (Chapel Hill: 1959), 335-37.

To William B. Giles
  December 31, 1795

. . . Were parties here divided merely by a greediness for office, as in England, to take a part with either would be unworthy of a reasonable or moral man, but where the principle of difference is as substantial and as strongly pronounced as between the republicans and the Monocrats of our country, I hold it as honorable to take a firm and decided part, and as immoral to pursue a middle line, as between the parties of Honest men, and Rogues, into which every country is divided.

To John Taylor
  June 4, 1798

. . . Our present situation is not a natural one. The body of our countrymen is substantially republican through every part of the Union. It was the irresistable influence and popularity of General Washington, played off by the cunning of Hamilton, which turned the government over to anti-republican hands, or turned the republican members, chosen by the people, into anti-republicans. He delivered it over to his successor in this state, and very untoward events, since improved with great artifice, have produced on the public mind the impression we see; but still, I repeat it, this is not the natural state. Time alone would bring round an order of things more correspondent to the sentiments of our constituents. . . . Be this as it may, in every free and deliberating society there must, from the nature of man, be opposite parties and violent dissensions and discords; and one of these, for the most part, must prevail over the other for a longer or shorter time. Perhaps this party division is necessary to induce each to watch and delate to the people the proceedings of the other. But if on a temporary superiority of the one party, the other is to resort to a scission of the Union, no federal government can ever exist. If to rid ourselves of the present rule of Massachusets and Connecticut we break the Union, will the evil stop there? Suppose the New England States alone cut off, will our natures be changed? are we not men still to the south of that, and with all the passions of men? Immediately we shall see a Pennsylvania and a Virginia party arise in the residuary confederacy, and the public mind will be distracted with the same party spirit. What a game, too, will the one party have in their hands by eternally threatening the other that unless they do so and so, they will join their Northern neighbors. If we reduce our Union to Virginia and North Carolina, immediately the conflict will be established between the representatives of these two States, and they will end by breaking into their simple units. Seeing, therefore, that an association of men who will not quarrel with one another is a thing which never yet existed, from the greatest confederacy of nations down to a town meeting or a vestry, seeing that we must have somebody to quarrel with, I had rather keep our New England associates for that purpose than to see our bickerings transferred to others. . . .

To John Wise
  February 12, 1798

I have duly received yours of the 28th Ultimo mentioning that it had been communicated to you, that in a conversation in Francis's Hotel (where I lodge) I had spoken of you as of Tory politics; and you make inquiry as to the fact and the "idea to be conveyed." I shall answer you with frankness. It is now well understood that two political Sects have arisen within the U. S. the one believing that the executive is the branch of our government which the most needs support; the other that like the analogous branch in the English Government, it is already too strong for the republican parts of the constitution; and therefore in equivocal cases they incline to the legislative powers: the former of these are called federalists, sometimes aristocrats or monocrats, and sometimes tories, after the corresponding sect in the English Government of exactly the same definition: the latter are stiled republicans, whigs, jacobins, anarchists, disorganizers etc. These terms are in familiar use with most persons, and which of those of the first class, I used on the occasion alluded to, I do not particularly remember; they are all well understood to designate persons who are for strengthening the executive rather than the legislative branches of the Government; but probably I used the last of those terms, and for these reasons: both parties claim to be federalists and republicans, and I believe with truth as to the great mass of them; these appellations therefore designate neither exclusively, and all the others are slanders, except those of whig and tory which alone characterise the distinguishing principles of the two Sects as I have before explained them; as they have been known and named in England for more than a century and as they are growing into daily use here with those, whose respect for the right of private Judgment in others, as well as themselves, does not permit them to use the other terms which either imply against themselves or charge others injuriously.

To William Short
November 10, 1804

The party division in this country is certainly not among it's pleasant features. To a certain degree it will always exist: and chiefly in mercantile places. In the country in those states where the republicans have a decided superiority, party hostility has ceased to infest society. But in those states where the parties are nearly equal the bitterness is in it's paroxysm. This is especially the case in Connecticut Massachusets and New Hampshire where the Federalists have still the majority but see that they must lose it in a trial or two more. . . . If the federalists would have been contented with my giving a very moderate participation in office to those who had been totally excluded, I had hoped to have been able to effect a reconciliation, and would sincerely have attempted it. But they spurned every overture of conciliation. I have therefore long since given up the idea, and proceed in all things without caring what they will think, say or do. To me will have fallen the drudgeory of putting them out of condition to do mischief. My successor I hope will have smoother seas. . . .

To John Adams
June 27, 1813

. . . Men have differed in opinion, and been divided into parties by these opinions, from the first origin of societies; and in all governments where they have been permitted freely to think and to speak. The same political parties which now agitate the U. S. have existed thro' all time. Whether the power of the people, or that of the aristocrats should prevail, were questions which kept the states of Greece and Rome in eternal convulsions; as they now schismatize every people whose minds and mouths are not shut up by the gag of a despot. And in fact the terms of whig and tory belong to natural, as well as to civil history. They denote the temper and constitution of mind of different individuals. To come to our own country, and to the times when you and I became first acquainted, we well remember the violent parties which agitated the old Congress, and their bitter contests. There you and I were together, and the Jays, and the Dickinsons, and other anti-independants were arrayed against us. They cherished the monarchy of England; and we the rights of our countrymen. When our present government was in the mew, passing from Confederation to Union, how bitter was the schism between the Feds and Antis. Here you and I were together again. . . . But as soon as it was put into motion, the line of division was again drawn, we broke into two parties, each wishing to give a different direction to the government; the one to strengthen the most popular branch, the other the more permanent branches, and to extend their permanence. Hence you and I separated for the first time: and as we had been longer than most others on the public theatre, and our names therefore were more familiar to our countrymen, the party which considered you as thinking with them, placed your name at their head; the other, for the same reason, selected mine. . . .

. . . To me then it appears that there have been differences of opinion, and party differences, from the first establishment of governments, to the present day; and on the same question which now divides our own country: that these will continue thro' all future time: that every one takes his side in favor of the many, or of the few, according to his constitution, and the circumstances in which he is placed: that opinions, which are equally honest on both sides, should not affect personal esteem, or social intercourse. . . .

6   JOHN TAYLOR ON PARTIES

John Taylor, of Caroline County, Virginia, philosopher of agrarian republicanism, regarded parties as the product of private interests and refused to accept the idea that parties were the natural result of free societies. [John Taylor], *A Definition of Parties* (Philadelphia: 1794), 2, 15; "Letters of John Taylor," *John P. Branch Historical Papers of Randolph-Macon College*, II (1905-8), 271-72; John Taylor, *An Inquiry into the Principles and Policy of the Government of the United States* [1814] (New Haven: 1950), 560-62.

A Definition of Parties, 1794

The existence of two parties in Congress is apparent. The fact is disclosed almost upon every important question. Whether the subject be foreign or domestic—relative to war or peace—navigation or commerce—the magnetism of opposite views draws them wide as the poles asunder. The situation of the public good, in the hands of two parties nearly poised as to numbers, must be extremely perilous. Truth is a thing, not of divisibility into conflicting parts, but of unity. Hence both sides cannot be right. Every patriot deprecates a disunion, which is only to be obviated by a national preference of one of these parties. It has therefore become as necessary, as it is difficult, to explore the causes of a political appearance, so baneful to the commonwealth. . . .

. . . It is indeed asserted, that a spirit of bigotry, is the cause of mischief. Upon that hypothesis, how happens it, that the faction cannot be defined, by any geographical boundary? It is also said, that the paper system has produced a real dissimilarity of interest among the several states? Why then is it, that the particles compounding the faction, are not united by the element of state interest, pervading an entire representation.

If either hypothesis had been true, a necessity for traversing the union from one extremity to the other, in search of the component parts of this faction, would not have existed. A necessity, which incontrovertibly proves, that neither geographical or state interests, have engendered this deadly foe to republicanism; but that it has been fostered by a private interest, confined in every state, to an inconsiderable number of citizens, and even largely shared by foreigners. If this is true, it is beyond calculation, to distinguish any material difference, in the degree of calamity, which it will inflict upon the states respectively.

Taylor to Jefferson
June 25, 1798

The party spirit amongst us is geographical or personal. If geographical, its superiority in either hemisphere, will beget the insolence of tyranny and the misery of slavery. A fluctuation of this superiority, will enlist revenge as an auxiliary passion, and annihilate the chance for human happiness.

If our party spirit is personal, it must arise from interest. This interest proceeds also from some cause. If the evil is in human nature, it may yet admit of alleviations. But if it springs from political encouragement, it is the work of art, and by art may be counteracted.

That parties, sufficiently malignant to destroy the public good, are not naturally the issue of every popular government, seems to be evinced by the examples of the state governments, and particularly by the eminent example of Connecticut, which has about two centuries enjoyed a compleat unanimity under a government, the most democratic of any representative form which ever existed. And that parties may be artificially produced, the scheme of balancing power against power, is equally evinced by the example of England. It is not possible, that one great error has been an initiation of the latter precedent, by counterpoising power against power, instead of securing to liberty an ascendant over power, whether simple or complex.

What are checks and balances, but party and faction? If a good form of government too often fails, in making bad men good, a bad form of government will too often succeed in making good men bad. Activity can only be bestowed upon these checks and balances by the exhibition of a prize. The prize can only consist of public property. This activity is then no evidence that a constitution has staked its existence upon the existence of faction and party and that it ensures their existence by purchasing it with public rights and wealth. . . .

If the mass of our citizens are now republican, will submission to antirepublican measures, increase that Mass? Where are the converts made during the late eventful periods by this policy? Has it not already lost the advantage of the locality of political opinion in some degree? A fact, which violently opposes the idea, that party spirit is simply the child of nature, and evidently refers origin to artifice and management. . . .

For it is my poor impression both that parties sufficiently malignant [to] end in political exacerbation are not natural to a republican government really dependent on natural will, and also that there is nothing supernatural in the party paroxysm which now exists. . . .

. . . Is it natural for all republicks to be divided upon fundamental principles? May not art and corruption produce such a division? Is man's natural propensity for liberty a sufficient curb upon this art and corruption? Monarchy will answer these questions. And let it prove, if it can, that an union in political principle is natural to man under a monarchy, but unnatural, under a republic. Of this I must doubt, until I see a republick so organized by annual and rotary officers—by breaking the entail of tax laws —and by equal representation, as to retain for the people, a real influence over the government. Constitutional paper vetos, are nothing, compared with a solid check, so woven into the form of government, as to be incapable of a separation from it.

*An Inquiry into the Principles and Policy
of the Government of the United States,* 1814

The danger of parties to free governments, arises from the impossibility of controlling them by the restraints of political law; because being constituted upon selfish views, like a set of mountebanks combined to administer drugs for the sake of getting fees, the nature of the poison cannot be foreseen, nor an effectual antidote anticipated. No division of power, no responsibility, no periodical change of leaders, no limitation of "thus far you may go and no farther," stops their career. In every form, therefore, they constitute the same avaricious or furious species of aristocracy, which would be produced by a form of government in the hands of a self constituted and uncontrolled body of men. They are universally disposed to persecute, plunder, oppress and kill, like all governments unsubjected to political law; and under the title of patriots, are, like fanaticks under the title of saints, ready to perpetrate any crimes to gratify their interest or prejudices. By melting down the fetters of moral and republican principles in party confidence, we abolish the only known remedy against the evil qualities of human nature, abandon our experiment of political law founded in these principles, and rest for security on ignorant mobs, guided by a few designing leaders, or on cunning combinations, guided by avarice and ambition. The Independents of England and the Jacobins of France, even abhorred the despotisms they introduced, but the results were unavoidable, as the natural effect of the unlimited confidence these parties acquired. This confidence produces an unlimited government, or one unrestricted by the ligatures of a moral analysis; and such a government is despotick. Under a despotism of any form, and in the form of a party of interest more than in any other, bodily safety, the safety of property, and the freedom of the mind, cease. Malice, envy and calumny instantly become the prime ministers of the furious and tottering tyrant. Knowing his doom from the fate of his predecessors, he hastens to glut his appetite for mischief before he dies. No numerical checks or balances can reach this dreadful party tyranny. It is even able to suspend or destroy those solemnly established by nations, and to make the people themselves the authors of their own ruin. . . . In legislation contrary to genuine republican principles, sustained by a dominant party zeal, lies, in my view, the greatest danger to the free form of government of the United States. . . .

7 IN DEFENSE OF PARTIES

Robert Goodloe Harper, a South Carolina Federalist, took an exceptional view of political parties. In this speech in the House of

Representatives, January 19, 1798, he went so far as to suggest that the opposing forces of party could produce a middle course of action in the public interest. *Annals of Congress,* 5th Congress, 2nd Session, 873-74.

Mr. Harper said he would now advert to another position advanced by the gentleman from Pennsylvania, (Mr. Gallatin,) and founded on a total misrepresentation of what he, Mr. Harper, had stated when he first spoke upon this question. . . . That gentleman, on the present occasion, had represented him as having attributed the opposition to Executive measures in that House to the anger which gentlemen felt at the disappointment of their hopes of obtaining offices; and he had then gone on to infer that the hope of obtaining offices must also influence the conduct of those members who usually supported the measures of the Executive; since, if disappointment in the pursuit of office could produce opposition, it was equally fair to attribute a contrary conduct in other members to the hope of succeeding in this pursuit. But Mr. Harper affirmed that he had said no such thing; that he had never attributed the opposition to this motive. He had indeed said, that the suspicions of gentlemen, and their clamors about Executive influence, patronage, and corruption, proceeded from disappointment, but not from disappointment of this kind. Ambitious statesmen, he said, did not wish for office, but power; they did not wish to hold posts themselves, but to direct those who did hold them; to see their own system adopted, their own advice followed, and the affairs of the country conducted in the way which they approved. This was their aim, and this the scope and end of all their exertions. While men should continue to think differently on matters of opinion, there would always be a number of persons who would disapprove the manner in which public affairs, or any other affairs, were conducted. These persons, in Governments like ours, would gradually form themselves into a party, and their opinions would assume the shape of a political system, different from that actually adopted. These two systems would be in a perpetual state of conflict, and the supporters of that which might happen to be vanquished, would feel mortification and chagrin. These feelings would become more and more violent in proportion as their defeats were more frequent, and on questions to which they annexed greater importance; and hence proceeded, and always would proceed, those heart-burnings and jealousies, those little suspicions which gave themselves vent in declamations against the opposite system and its supporters, against Executive influence, against patronage and corruption, and whereby the party which could not rule was prompted to suspect and arraign the motives which actuated the authors of their defeat. Such were the passions and such the feelings to which he attributed the opposition of gentlemen and their little unfounded suspicions: to a love of power, not to a love of place; to disappointment in their attempts to bring their own system and their own principles into action, not to the pursuit of office. . . .

It was not, therefore, to the disappointment of gentlemen in the pursuit of those objects, Mr. Harper said, that he attributed their conduct, but to the usual operations of party spirit which arose out of the constitution of our nature, combined with the form of our Government; and of which he did not complain. He not only knew that it must exist while men should be made as they are, but he believed that it ought to exist. While opposite parties in the Government struggled for pre-eminence, they were like persons engaged in an exhibition before the public, who are obliged to display superior merit and superior excellence in order to gain the prize. The public is the judge, the two parties are the combatants, and that party which possesses power must employ it properly, must conduct the Government wisely, in order to insure public approbation, and retain their power. In this contention, while the two parties draw different ways, a middle course is produced generally conformable to public good. Party spirit, therefore, and the contentions to which it gave rise, neither alarmed nor displeased him. It might, indeed, sometimes run into excess, and produce mischief, as the wind may sometimes be converted into a storm, or fire give rise to a conflagration; but its general effects, like those of the great elements of nature, he had no doubt, were beneficial.

8   JAMES HILLHOUSE SPEAKS ON PARTIES

A Connecticut Federalist, Senator Hillhouse saw clearly that presidential elections had contributed much to the formation of national parties and, indeed, that presidential elections were not being conducted as the framers of the Constitution had envisaged. One of the proposals he made to reverse the party trend was to amend the Constitution to choose the President annually by lot among the members of the Senate. Hillhouse was speaking on this subject when he made the following remarks in the Senate, April 12, 1808. *Annals of Congress,* 10th Congress, 1st Session, 344-46.

Party spirit is the demon which engendered the faction that have destroyed most free governments. State or local parties will have but a feeble influence on the General Government. Regular, organized parties only, extending from the northern to the southern extremity of the United States, and from the Atlantic to the utmost western limits, threaten to shake this Union to its centre. No man can be so blind but he must see, and the fact is too notorious to be denied, that such parties have commenced in this country, and are progressing with gigantic strides. The danger is great, and demands an early and decisive remedy. There is but one, which presents itself to my mind; this is, to cut off the head of the demon. For without a head, without a rallying point, no dangerous party can be formed, no such party can exist. There is but a single point in the Constitution, which can be made to bear upon all the States at one and the same time, and produce a unity of interest and action, and thus serve as the rallying point of party; and that is the Presidential election. This most dignified and important office of President, made more desirable by having attached to it a high salary, great power, and extensive patronage; cannot fail to bring forth and array all the electioneering artillery of the country; and furnish the most formidable means of organizing, concentrating, and cementing parties. And when a President shall be elected by means of party influence, thus powerfully exerted, he cannot avoid party bias, and will thence become the chief of a party, instead of taking the dignified attitude of a President of the United States. If some other mode of filling the Presidential chair, than that of a general election throughout the United States, were devised and adopted, it would be impossible to form national parties. There would in some instances be State and local parties, but they would have a very inconsiderable effect on the General Government; they would be like town or county parties in States, which have a limited operation on the councils of the State. Indeed this Presidential election does more than anything else towards making parties in States—parties dangerous to their ancient institutions, and producing an injurious effect upon their most important concerns. In one word, it is now manifest, that the present mode of electing a President is producing, and will produce, many and great evils to the Union, and to the individual States.

The framers of the Constitution were, I am told, strongly impressed with a sense of the difficulties and dangers which would attend a Presidential election, and hence the various projects which were offered, considered, and rejected. But to prevent a total failure of the object of their convening, they finally adopted the novel and complicated mode contained in the Constitution: calculating upon it as a mode that would secure a fair, unbiassed exercise of the right of suffrage. To guard against official and Congressional influence, the electors were to be chosen in each State, of whom no member of Congress or officer of the United States was to be one. To prevent combinations among the States, there was allowed but a short interval between the time of their being elected and that of giving in their votes. To prevent cabal among the electors, they were to meet in their respective States, and give in their votes on the same day. To guard against

State attachments, two persons were to be voted for as President, one of whom at least was not to be of the same State with themselves. And to insure a fair canvass of the votes, they were to be opened, and the election declared, in the presence of both Houses of Congress: the person having the greatest number of votes, if a majority of the whole number of electors appointed, to be President; and if more than one have such majority, and have an equal number of votes, the House of Representatives to choose by ballot one of them for President: if no one have a majority, then, out of the five highest, the House of Representatives in like manner to choose a President. In both cases the votes are to be taken by States, the representatives from each State having one vote. This mode, so beautiful in theory, has substantially failed in practice.

The ingenuity of man being great, is it not to be feared that the time will come, and would it not be cause of deep regret if the time should come, when the country shall be so divided into parties, that a small number of persons, and those exclusively members of Congress, (who are intended by the Constitution to be excluded from all intermeddling in Presidential elections,) and that too in the very focus of Presidential and official influence, (which the Constitution meant carefully to guard against,) shall nominate a President? And to secure his election, it will be required that every person before he shall receive a vote or an appointment as an elector, shall pledge himself to support such nomination; and thus the President will in fact be made to choose the electors, instead of the electors choosing the President. . . .

Of the impropriety and impolicy of the present mode of electing a President, can there be stronger proof, can there be a more convincing evidence, than is now exhibiting in the United States? In whatever direction we turn our eyes, we behold the people arranging themselves under the banners of different candidates, for the purpose of commencing the electioneering campaign for the next President and Vice President. All the passions and feelings of the human heart are brought into the most active operation. The electioneering spirit finds its way to every fireside; pervades our domestic circles; and threatens to destroy the enjoyment of social harmony. The seeds of discord will be sown in families, among friends, and throughout the whole community. . . .

II ISSUES AND IDEOLOGIES OF EARLY PARTY CONFLICT

Many issues—national, state, and local—affected the emergence of national political parties in the United States, but national issues clearly predominated. Congressional actions and executive policies in organizing the new government under the Constitution and fashioning its domestic and foreign policies gave rise to issues that influenced American politics from presidential elections to the selection of local sheriffs. Congress, more than anywhere else, became the center from which party conflict spread throughout the Union.

During the formative first decade of the American party system, the financial program of Secretary of the Treasury Alexander Hamilton generated major domestic disputes, while problems growing out of the French Revolution and the ensuing wars in Europe precipitated critical controversies over foreign relations. The Jay Treaty with Great Britain, one of the most divisive issues of Washington's two terms, gave great momentum to partisan conflict. The responses of John Adams's administration to the threat of war with France—the expansion of the military establishment and the accompanying domestic policy embodied in the alien and sedition laws —were the major issues of the presidential election of 1800.

Party ideology was always related to specific circumstances and issues, and contemporaries did not separate ideology from policy in their discussions of current issues. Yet some party participants, of whom Jefferson is an outstanding example, were given to the exposition of principles and the formulation of broad concepts of purpose. In numerous letters written during the years of Republican opposition, Jefferson expounded the basic political creed which he later reaffirmed in his first inaugural address. As long as they were in power and the burden of justifying change fell to the opposition, Federalist leaders were less given to theorizing than the Republicans; but in the wake of their defeat in 1800, Federalists, such as Robert Goodloe Harper, also sought to explain their basic purposes.

9 THOMAS JEFFERSON ON THE
CONSTITUTIONALITY OF A NATIONAL BANK

Funding measures and the assumption of state debts created sharp divisions in Congress, but the chartering of the Bank of the United States was the most controversial of Hamilton's proposals to be enacted. The bank bill crystallized Jefferson's wariness of Hamilton into positive opposition. Before signing the act, President Washington requested written opinions on its constitutionality from Hamilton, Secretary of State Jefferson, and Attorney General Edmund Randolph. Jefferson advanced the arguments of strict construction in a concise brief, February 15, 1791. Ford, ed., *Writings of Thomas Jefferson,* V, 284-89.

I consider the foundation of the Constitution as laid on this ground: That "all powers not delegated to the United States, by the Constitution, nor prohibited by it to the States, are reserved to the States or to the People." To take a single step beyond the boundaries thus specially drawn around the powers of Congress, is to take possession of a boundless field of power, no longer susceptible of any definition.

The incorporation of a bank, and the powers assumed by this bill, have not, in my opinion, been delegated to the United States, by the Constitution.

I. They are not among the powers specially enumerated: for these are: 1st. A power to lay taxes for the purpose of paying the debts of the United States; but no debt is paid by this bill, nor any tax laid. Were it a bill to raise money, its origination in the Senate would condemn it by the Constitution.

2d. "To borrow money." But this bill neither borrows money nor ensures the borrowing it. The proprietors of the bank will be just as free as any other money holders, to lend or not to lend their money to the public. The operation proposed in the bill, first, to lend them two millions, and then to borrow them back again, cannot change the nature of the latter act, which will still be a payment, and not a loan, call it by what name you please.

3. To "regulate commerce with foreign nations, and among the States, and with the Indian tribes." To erect a bank, and to regulate commerce, are very different acts. He who erects a bank, creates a subject of commerce in its bills; so does he who makes a bushel of wheat, or digs a dollar out of the mines; yet neither of these persons regulates commerce thereby. To make a thing which may be bought and sold, is not to prescribe regulations for buying and selling. Besides, if this was an exercise of the power of regu-

lating commerce, it would be void, as extending as much to the internal commerce of every State, as to its external. For the power given to Congress by the Constitution does not extend to the internal regulation of the commerce of a State, (that is to say of the commerce between citizen and citizen,) which remain exclusively with its own legislature; but to its external commerce only, that is to say, its commerce with another State, or with foreign nations, or with the Indian tribes. Accordingly the bill does not propose the measure as a regulation of trade, but as "productive of considerable advantages to trade." Still less are these powers covered by any other of the special enumerations.

II. Nor are they within either of the general phrases, which are the two following:

1. To lay taxes to provide for the general welfare of the United States, that is to say, "to lay taxes for *the purpose* of providing for the general welfare." For the laying of taxes is the *power,* and the general welfare the *purpose* for which the power is to be exercised. They are not to lay taxes *ad libitum for any purpose they please;* but only *to pay the debts or provide for the welfare of the Union.* In like manner, they are not *to do anything they please* to provide for the general welfare, but only to *lay taxes* for that purpose. To consider the latter phrase, not as describing the purpose of the first, but as giving a distinct and independent power to do any act they please, which might be for the good of the Union, would render all the preceding and subsequent enumerations of power completely useless.

It would reduce the whole instrument to a single phrase, that of instituting a Congress with power to do whatever would be for the good of the United States; and, as they would be the sole judges of the good or evil, it would be also a power to do whatever evil they please.

It is an established rule of construction where a phrase will bear either of two meanings, to give it that which will allow some meaning to the other parts of the instrument, and not that which would render all the others useless. Certainly no such universal power was meant to be given them. It was intended to lace them up straitly within the enumerated powers, and those without which, as means, these powers could not be carried into effect. It is known that the very power now proposed *as a means* was rejected as *an end* by the Convention which formed the Constitution. A proposition was made to them to authorize Congress to open canals, and an amendatory one to empower them to incorporate. But the whole was rejected, and one of the reasons for rejection urged in debate was, that then they would have a power to erect a bank, which would render the great cities, where there were prejudicies and jealousies on the subject, adverse to the reception of the Constitution.

2. The second general phrase is, "to make all laws *necessary* and proper for carrying into execution the enumerated powers." But they can all be carried into execution without a bank. A bank therefore is not *necessary,* and consequently not authorized by this phrase.

It has been urged that a bank will give great facility or convenience in the collection of taxes. Suppose this were true: yet the Constitution allows only the means which are *"necessary,"* not those which are merely "convenient" for effecting the enumerated powers. If such a latitude of construction be allowed to this phrase as to give any non-enumerated power, it will go to every one, for there is not one which ingenuity may not torture into a *convenience* in some instance *or other,* to *some one* of so long a list of enumerated powers. It would swallow up all the delegated powers, and reduce the whole to one power, as before observed. Therefore it was that the Constitution restrained them to the *necessary* means, that is to say, to those means without which the grant of power would be nugatory. . . .

Perhaps, indeed, bank bills may be a more *convenient* vehicle than treasury orders. But a little *difference* in the degree of *convenience,* cannot constitute the necessity which the constitution makes the ground for assuming any non-enumerated power. . . .

It may be said that a bank whose bills would have a currency all over the States, would be more convenient than one whose currency is limited to a single State. So it would be still more convenient that there should be a bank, whose bills should have a currency all over the world. But it does not follow from this superior conveniency, that there exists anywhere a power to establish such a bank; or that the world may not go on very well without it. . . .

The negative of the President is the shield provided by the constitution to protect against the invasions of the legislature: 1. The right of the Executive. 2. Of the Judiciary. 3. Of the States and State legislatures. The present is the case of a right remaining exclusively with the States, and consequently one of those intended by the Constitution to be placed under its protection.

It must be added, however, that unless the President's mind on a view of everything which is urged for and against this bill, is tolerably clear that it is unauthorised by the Constitution; if the pro and the con hang so even as to balance his judgment, a just respect for the wisdom of the legislature would naturally decide the balance in favor of their opinion. It is chiefly for cases where they are clearly misled by error, ambition, or interest, that the Constitution has placed a check in the negative of the President.

10 ALEXANDER HAMILTON ON THE CONSTITUTIONALITY OF A NATIONAL BANK

When he wrote his opinion, February 23, 1791, Hamilton had before him the opinions of Jefferson and Randolph. His defense of the bank as constitutional advanced a classic exposition of the doctrine of implied powers. Richard B. Morris, ed., *Alexander Hamilton and the Founding of the Nation* (New York: 1957), 263-68.

In entering upon the argument, it ought to be premised that the Objections of the Secretary of State and the Attorney General are founded on a general denial of the authority of the United States to erect corporations. The latter, indeed, expressly admits, that if there be anything in the bill which is not warranted by the Constitution, it is the clause of incorporation.

Now it appears to the Secretary of the Treasury that this *general principle* is *inherent* in the very *definition* of government, and *essential to* every step of the progress to be made by that of the United States, namely: That every power vested in a government is in its nature *sovereign,* and includes, by *force* of the *term,* a right to employ all the *means* requisite and fairly applicable to the attainment of the *ends* of such power, and which are not precluded by restrictions and exceptions specified in the Constitution, or not immoral, or not contrary to the *essential ends* of political society. . . .

If it would be necessary to bring proof to a proposition so clear, as that which affirms that the powers of the Federal Government, as to *its objects,* are sovereign, there is a clause of its Constitution which would be decisive. It is that which declares that the Constitution, and the laws of the United States made in pursuance of it, and all treaties made, or which shall be made, under their authority, shall be the *supreme law of the land.* The power which can create the *supreme law* of the land in any case, is doubtless sovereign as to such case.

This general and indisputable principle puts at once an end to the abstract question, whether the United States have power to erect a *corporation;* that is to say, to give a *legal* or *artificial Capacity* to one or more persons, distinct from the *natural.* For it is unquestionably incident to *Sovereign Power* to erect corporations, and consequently to that of the United States, in *relation* to the *objects* intrusted to the management of the government. The difference is this: where the authority of the government is general, it can create corporations in *all* cases; where it is confined to certain branches of legislation, it can create corporations only in those cases. . . .

It is not denied that there are *implied,* as well as *express* powers, and that the former are as effectually delegated as the latter. And for the sake of accuracy it shall be mentioned that there is another class of powers, which may be properly denominated resulting powers. It will not be doubted that if the United States should make a conquest of any of the territories of its neighbors, they would possess sovereign jurisdiction over the conquered territory. This would rather be a result from the whole mass of the powers of the government, and from the nature of political society, than a consequence of either of the powers specially enumerated. . . .

It is conceded that *implied powers* are to be considered as delegated equally with *express ones.* Then it follows, that as a power of erecting a corporation may as well be *implied* as any other thing, it may as well be employed as an *instrument* or *means* of carrying into execution any of the specified powers, as any other *instrument* or *mean* whatever. The only question must be in this, as in every other case, whether the *mean* to be employed, or, in this instance, the corporation to be erected, has a natural relation to any of the acknowledged objects or lawful ends of the government. Thus a corporation may not be erected by Congress for superintending the police of the city of Philadelphia, because they are not authorized to *regulate* the *police* of that city. But one may be erected in relation to the collection of taxes, or to the trade with foreign countries, or to the trade between the States, or with the Indian tribes, because it is the province of the Federal Government to *regulate* those objects, and because it is incident to a general *sovereign* or legislative power to *regulate* a thing, to employ all the means which relate to its regulation to the best and greatest advantage. . . .

To this mode of reasoning respecting the right of employing all the means requisite to the execution of the specified powers of the government, it is objected, that none but necessary and proper means are to be employed; and the Secretary of State maintains, that no means are to be considered *necessary* but those without which the grant of the power would be *nugatory.* . . .

It is essential to the being of the national government, that so erroneous a conception of the meaning of the word *necessary* should be exploded. It is certain, that neither the grammatical nor popular sense of the term requires that construction. According to both, *necessary* often means no more than *needful, requisite, incidental, useful,* or *conducive to.* It is a common mode of expression to say, that it is *necessary* for a government or a person to do this or that thing, when nothing more is intended or understood, than that the interests of the government or person require, or will be promoted by, the doing of this or that thing. The imagination can be at no loss for exemplifications of the use of the word in this sense. And it is the true one in which it is to be understood as used in the Constitution. The whole turn of the clause containing it indicates, that it was the intent of the Convention, by that clause, to give a liberal latitude to the exercise of the specified powers. The expressions have peculiar comprehensiveness. They are, "to make all *laws* necessary and proper for *carrying into execution* the foregoing powers, and all *other powers* vested by the Constitution in the *Government* of the United States, or in any *department* or *Officer* thereof."

To understand the word as the Secretary of State does, would be to depart from its obvious and popular sense, and to give it a *restrictive* operation, an idea never before entertained. It would be to give it the same force as if the word *absolutely* or *indispensably* had been prefixed to it. . . .

The *degree* in which a measure is necessary can never be a *test* of the legal right to adopt it; that must be a matter of opinion, and can only be a *test* of expediency. The *relation* between the *measure* and the *end;* between the *nature* of the *mean* employed towards the execution of a power, and the object of that power, must be the criterion of constitutionality, not the more or less of *necessity* or *utility.* . . .

This restrictive interpretation of the word *necessary* is also contrary to this sound maxim of construction; namely, that the powers contained in a constitution of government, especially those which concern the general administration of the affairs of a country, its finances, trade, defence, etc., ought to be construed liberally in advancement of the public good. This rule does not depend on the particular form of a government, or on the particular demarcation of the boundaries of its powers, but on the nature and objects of government itself. The means by which national exigencies are to be provided for, national inconveniences obviated, national prosperity promoted, are of such infinite variety, extent, and complexity, that there must of necessity be great latitude of discretion in the selection and application of those means. Hence, consequently, the necessity and propriety of exercising the authorities intrusted to a government on principles of liberal construction. . . .

But the doctrine which is contended for is not chargeable with the consequences imputed to it. It does not affirm that the National Government is sovereign in all respects, but that it is sovereign to a certain extent—that is, to the extent of the objects of its specified powers.

It leaves, therefore, a criterion of what is constitutional, and of what is not so. This criterion is the *end,* to which the measure relates as a *mean.* If the *end* be clearly comprehended within any of the specified powers, and if the measure have an obvious relation to that *end,* and is not forbidden by any particular provision of the Constitution, it may safely be deemed to come within the compass of the national authority. There is also this further criterion, which may materially assist the decision: Does the proposed measure abridge a pre-existing right of any State or of any individual? If it does not, there is a strong presumption in favor of its constitutionality, and slighter relations to any declared object of the Constitution may be permitted to turn the scale. . . .

It is presumed to have been satisfactorily shown in the Course of the preceding observations:

1. That the power of the government, *as* to the objects intrusted to its management, is, in its nature, sovereign.

2. That the right of erecting corporations is one inherent in, and inseparable from, the idea of sovereign power.

3. That the position, that the government of the United States can exercise no power but such as is delegated to it by its Constitution, does not militate against this principle.

4. That the word *necessary,* in the general clause, can have no *restrictive* operation derogating from the force of this principle; indeed, that the degree in which a measure is or is not *necessary,* cannot be a *test* of *constitutional right,* but of *expediency* only.

5. That the power to erect corporations is not to be considered as an *independent* and *substantive* power, but as an *incidental* and *auxiliary* one, and was therefore more properly left to implication, than expressly granted.

6. That the principle in question does not extend the power of the government beyond the prescribed limits, because it only affirms a power to *incorporate* for purposes within the *sphere* of the *specified powers.*

And lastly, that the right to exercise such a power in certain cases is unequivocally granted in the most *positive* and *comprehensive* terms. . . .

To establish such a right, it remains to show the relation of such an institution to one or more of the specified powers of the government. Accordingly it is affirmed that it has a relation, more or less direct, to the power of collecting taxes, to that of borrowing money, to that of regulating trade between the States, and to those of raising and maintaining fleets and armies. To the two former, the relation may be said to be immediate; and in the last place it will be argued, that it is clearly within the provision which authorizes the making of all *needful rules* and *regulations* concerning the *property* of the United States, as the same has been practised upon by the government. . . .

Under a conviction that such a relation subsists, the Secretary of the Treasury, with all deference, conceives that it will result as a necessary consequence from the position, that all the specified powers of government are sovereign, as to the proper objects; that the incorporation of a bank is a constitutional measure; and that the objections taken to the bill, in this respect, are ill-founded. . . .

11 A REPUBLICAN NEWSPAPER
VIEWS PARTY DIFFERENCES

The Philadelphia *National Gazette,* April 30, 1792, presented a brief Republican view of economic and constitutional principles underlying party conflict.

Two parties, says a correspondent, have shewn themselves in the doings of the new government. One have evidently thought favorably of a great public debt—whereas the other have viewed it as an evil, however necessary a one.

So also, one party have considered speculation as the very soul of public credit, and as the mark of useful enterprise and thriving wealth. The other, with a contrary eye, have viewed it as the pampered child of an unruly avarice, and the prolific parent of idleness, dissipation and fraud.

Further, it has been the endeavor of one party to work the public debt into an instrument for heaping up vast wealth in the hands of a few, so as by the subtle efficacy of monied influence, to divide and rule the many. The other have stood up against this kind of policy, as unjust and unrepublican, and as injurious to all the best interests of the country.

Again, one party have advocated the widest constructions of the Constitution, so as to carry the powers of the government far beyond the obvious intent and meaning thereof, and therefore beyond the grant of the people. The other have been of a different temper, and contended for a regular observance of the Constitution, equally where it limits as where it grants power, and for carrying it into execution in a republican spirit and manner.

12 HAMILTON DISCUSSES POLITICS
AND THE STATE OF PARTIES

In this detailed letter to Edward Carrington, of Virginia, May 26, 1792, Hamilton presents his case in the erupting party conflict. Discussing the opposition of Madison and Jefferson, examining their presumed motives, and answering the charges of alleged dangerous tendencies in Federalist policies, Hamilton makes his most revealing statement on the rise of parties. Henry Cabot Lodge, ed., *The Works of Alexander Hamilton* (Constitutional Edition, New York: [1904]), IX, 513-35.

Believing that I possess a share of your personal friendship and confidence, and yielding to that which I feel towards you; persuaded also, that our political creed is the same on two essential points—first, the necessity of Union to the respectability and happiness of this country, and second, the necessity of an efficient general government to maintain the Union, I have concluded to unbosom myself to you, on the present state of political parties and views. . . . When I accepted the office I now hold, it was under full persuasion, that from similarity of thinking, conspiring with personal good-will, I should have the firm support of Mr. Madison, in the general course of my administration. Aware of the intrinsic difficulties of the situation, and of the powers of Mr. Madison, I do not believe I should have accepted under a different supposition. I have mentioned the similarity of thinking between that gentleman and myself. This was relative, not merely to the general principles of national policy and government, but to the leading points, which were likely to constitute questions in the administration of the finances. I mean, first, the expediency of funding the debt; second, the inexpediency of discrimination between original and present holders; third, the expediency of assuming the State debts. . . .

Under these circumstances you will naturally imagine that it must have been matter of surprise to me when I was apprised that it was Mr. Madison's intention to oppose my plan on both the last-mentioned points. Before the debate commenced, I had a conversation with him on my report; in the course of which I alluded to the calculation I had made of his sentiments, and the grounds of that calculation. He did not deny them; but alleged in his justification that the very considerable alienation of the debt, subsequent to the periods at which he had opposed a discrimination, had essentially changed the state of the question; and that as to the assumption, he had contemplated it to take place as matters stood at the peace. . . .

At this time and afterwards repeated intimations were given to me that Mr. Madison, from a spirit of rivalship, or some other cause, had become personally unfriendly to me; and one gentleman in particular, whose honor I have no reason to doubt, assured me that Mr. Madison, in a conversation with him, had made a pretty direct attempt to insinuate unfavorable impressions of me. Still I suspended my opinion on the subject. I knew the malevolent officiousness of mankind too well to yield a very ready acquiescence to the suggestions which were made, and resolved to wait till time and more experience should afford a solution. It was not till the last session that I became unequivocally convinced of the following truth: "that Mr. Madison, co-operating with Mr. Jefferson, is at the head of a faction decidedly hostile to me and my administration; and actuated by views, in my judgment, subversive of the principles of good government and dangerous to the Union, peace, and happiness of the country."

These are strong expressions, they may pain your friendship for one or both of the gentlemen whom I have named. I have not lightly resolved to hazard them. They are the result of a serious alarm in my mind for the public welfare, and of a full conviction that what I have alleged is a truth, and a truth which ought to be told, and well attended to by all the friends of the Union and efficient national government. The suggestion will, I hope, at least, awaken attention free from the bias of former prepossessions.

This conviction, in my mind, is the result of a long train of circumstances, many of them minute. To attempt to detail them all would fill a volume. I shall therefore confine myself to the mention of a few.

First.—As to the point of opposition to me and my administration.

Mr. Jefferson, with very little reserve, manifests his dislike of the funding system generally, calling in question the expediency of funding a debt at all. Some expressions, which he has dropped in my presence (sometimes without sufficient attention to delicacy), will not permit me to doubt on this point representations which I have had from various respectable quarters. I do not mean that he advocates directly the undoing of what has been done, but he censures the whole, on principles which, if they should become general, could not but end in the subversion of the system. In various conversations, with foreigners as well as citizens, he has thrown censure on my principles of government and on my measures of administration. He has predicted that the people would not long tolerate my proceedings, and that I should not long maintain my ground. Some of those whom he immediately and notoriously moves have even whispered suspicions of the rectitude of my motives and conduct. In the question concerning the bank he not only delivered an opinion in writing against its constitutionality and expediency, but he did it in a style and manner which I felt as partaking of asperity and ill humor toward me. As one of the trustees of the sinking fund, I have experienced in almost every leading question opposition from him. When any turn of things in the community has threatened either odium or embarrassment to me, he has not been able to suppress the satisfaction which it gave him. A part of this is, of course, information, and might be misrepresentation, but it comes through so many channels, and so well accords with what falls under my own observation, that I can entertain no doubt.

I find a strong confirmation in the following circumstances: Freneau, the present printer of the *National Gazette,* who was a journeyman with Childs and Swain, at New York, was a known Anti-federalist. It is reduced to a certainty that he was brought to Philadelphia by Mr. Jefferson to be the conductor of a newspaper. It is notorious that contemporarily with the commencement of his paper he was a clerk in the Department of State, for foreign languages. Hence a clear inference that his paper has been set on foot and is conducted under the patronage and not against the views of Mr. Jefferson. What then is the complexion of this paper? Let any impartial man peruse all the numbers down to the present day, and I never was more mistaken if he does not pronounce that it is a paper devoted to the subversion of me and the measures in which I have had an agency; and I am little less mistaken if he does not pronounce that it is a paper of a tendency generally unfriendly to the government of the United States. . . .

With regard to Mr. Madison, the matter stands thus: I have not heard, but in the one instance to which I have alluded, of his having held language unfriendly to me in private conversation, but in his public conduct there has been a more uniform and persevering opposition than I have been able to resolve into a sincere difference of opinion. I cannot persuade myself that Mr. Madison and I, whose politics had formerly so much the same point of departure, should now diverge so widely in our opinions of the measures which are proper to be pursued. The opinion I once entertained of the candor and simplicity and fairness of Mr. Madison's character, has, I acknowledge, given way to a decided opinion that it is one of a peculiarly artificial and complicated kind. For a considerable part of the last session Mr. Madison lay in a great measure perdu. But it was evident from his votes and a variety of little movements and appearances, that he was the prompter of Mr. Giles and others who were the open instruments of the opposition. . . .

My overthrow was anticipated as certain, and Mr. Madison, laying aside his wonted caution, boldly led his troops, as he imagined, to a certain victory. He was disappointed. Though late, I became apprised of the danger. Measures of counteraction were adopted, and when the question was called Mr. Madison was confounded to find characters voting against him whom he counted upon as certain. Towards the close of the session another, though a more covert, attack was made. It was in the shape of a proposition to insert in the supplementary act respecting the public debt something by way of instruction to the trustees "to make their purchases of the debt at the lowest market price." In the course of the discussion of this point Mr. Madison dealt much in insidious insinuations calculated to give an impression that the public money, under my particular direction, had been unfaithfully applied to put undue advantages in the pockets of speculators, and to support the debt at an artificial price for their benefit. The whole manner of this transaction left no doubt in any one's mind that Mr. Madison was actuated by personal and political animosity. . . .

Secondly, as to the tendency of the views of the two gentlemen who have been named. Mr. Jefferson is an avowed enemy to a funded debt. Mr. Madison disavows, in public, any intention to undo what has been done, but, in private conversation with Mr. Charles Carroll, Senator, . . . he favored the sentiment in Mr. Mercer's speech, that a Legislature had no right to fund the debt by mortgaging permanently the public revenues, because they had no right to bind posterity. The inference is that what has been unlawfully done may be undone.

The discourse of partisans in the Legislature, and the publication in the party newspapers, direct their main battery against the principle of a funded debt, and represent it in the most odious light as a perfect Pandora's box. . . .

In almost all the questions, great and small, which have arisen since the first session of Congress, Mr. Jefferson and Mr. Madison have been found among those who are disposed to narrow the federal authority. The question of a national bank is one example. . . . On the militia bill, and in a variety of minor cases, he [i.e., Madison] has leaned to abridging the exercise of federal authority, and leaving as much as possible to the States; and he lost no opportunity of sounding the alarm, with great affected solemnity, at encroachments, meditated on the rights of the States, and of holding up the bugbear of a faction in the government having designs unfriendly to liberty.

. . . In respect to foreign politics, the views of these gentlemen are, in my judgment, equally unsound and dangerous. They have a womanish attachment to France and a womanish resentment against Great Britain. They would draw us into the closest embrace of the former, and involve us in all the consequences of her politics; and they would risk the peace of the country in their endeavors to keep us at the greatest possible distance from the latter. This disposition goes to a length, particularly in Mr. Jefferson, of which, till lately, I had no adequate idea. Various circumstances prove to me that if these gentlemen were left to pursue their own course, there would be, in less than six months, an open war between the United States and Great Britain. . . .

Another circumstance has contributed to widening the breach. 'T is evident, beyond a question, from every movement, that Mr. Jefferson aims with ardent desire at the Presidential chair. This, too, is an important object of the party-politics. It is supposed, from the nature of my former personal and political connections, that I may favor some other candidate more than Mr. Jefferson, when the question shall occur by the retreat of the present gentleman. My influence, therefore, with the community becomes a thing, on ambitious and personal grounds, to be resisted and destroyed. You know how much it was a point to establish the Secretary of State, as the officer who was to administer the government in defect of the President and Vice-President. Here, I acknowledge, though I took far less part than was supposed, I ran counter to Mr. Jefferson's wishes; but if I had had no other reason for it, I had already experienced opposition from him, which rendered it a measure of self-defence. It is possible, too, (for men easily heat their imaginations when their passions are heated,) that they have by degrees persuaded themselves of what they may have at first only sported to influence others, namely, that there is some dreadful combination against State government and republicanism; which, according to them, are convertible terms. But there is so much absurdity in this supposition, that the admission of it tends to apologize for their hearts at the expense of their heads. Under the influence of all these circumstances the attachment to the government of the United States, originally weak in Mr. Jefferson's mind, has given way to something very like dislike in Mr. Madison's. It is so counteracted by personal feelings as to be more an affair of the head than of the heart; more the result of a conviction of the necessity of Union than of cordiality to the thing itself. I hope it does not stand worse than this with him. In such a state of mind both these gentlemen are prepared to hazard a great deal to effect a change. Most of the important measures of every government are connected with the treasury. To subvert the present head of it, they deem it expedient to risk rendering the government itself odious; perhaps foolishly thinking that they can easily recover the lost affections and confidence of the people, and not appreciating, as they ought to do, the natural resistance to government, which in every community results from the human passions, the degree to which this is strengthened by the organized rivality of State governments, and the infinite danger that the national government, once rendered odious, will be kept so by these powerful and indefatigable enemies. . . .

A word on another point. I am told that serious apprehensions are disseminated in your State as to the existence of a monarchical party meditating the destruction of State and republican government. If it is possible that so absurd an idea can gain ground, it is necessary that it should be combated. I assure you, on my private faith and honor as a man, that there is not, in my judgment, a shadow of foundation for it. A very small number of men indeed may entertain theories less republican than Mr. Jefferson and Mr. Madison, but I am persuaded there is not a man among them who would not regard as both criminal and visionary any attempt to subvert the republican system of the country. Most of these men rather fear that it may not justify itself by its fruits, than feel a predilection for a different form; and their fears are not diminished by the factious and fanatical politics which they find prevailing among a certain set of gentlemen and threatening to disturb the tranquillity and order of the government.

As to the destruction of State governments, the great and real anxiety is to be able to preserve the national from the too potent and counteracting influence of those governments. As to my own political creed, I give it to you with the utmost sincerity. I am affectionately attached to the republican theory. I desire above all things to see the equality of political rights, exclusive of all hereditary distinction, firmly established by a practical demonstration of its being consistent with the order and happiness of society. As to State governments, the prevailing bias of my judgment is that if they can be circumscribed within bounds, consistent with the preservation of the national government, they will prove useful and salutary. If the States were all of the size of Connecticut, Maryland, or New Jersey, I should decidedly regard the local governments as both safe and useful. As the thing now is, however, I acknowledge the most serious apprehensions, that the government of the United States will not be able to maintain itself against their influence. I see that influence already penetrating into the national councils and preventing their direction. Hence, a disposition on my part towards a liberal construction of the powers of the national government, and to erect every fence, to guard it from depredations which is, in my opinion, consistent with constitutional propriety. As to any combination to prostrate the State governments, I disavow and deny it. From an apprehension lest the judiciary should not work efficiently or harmoniously, I have been desirous of seeing some national scheme of connection adopted as an amendment to the Constitution, otherwise I am for maintaining things as they are; though I doubt much the possibility of it, from a tendency in the nature of things towards the preponderancy of the State governments.

I said that I was affectionately attached to the republican theory. This is the real language of my heart, which I open to you in the sincerity of friendship; and I add that I have strong hopes of the success of that theory; but, in candor, I ought also to add that I am far from being without doubts. I consider its success as yet a problem. It is yet to be determined by experience whether it be consistent with that stability and order in government which are essential to public strength and private security and happiness.

On the whole, the only enemy which Republicanism has to fear in this country is in the spirit of faction and anarchy. If this will not permit the ends of government to be attained under it, if it engenders disorders in the community, all regular and orderly minds will wish for a change, and the demagogues who have produced the disorder will make it for their own aggrandizement. This is the old story. If I were disposed to promote monarchy and overthrow State governments, I would mount the hobby-horse of popularity; I would cry out "usurpation," "danger to liberty," etc., etc.; I would endeavor to prostrate the national government, raise a ferment, and then "ride in the whirlwind, and direct the storm." That there are men acting with Jefferson and Madison who have this in view, I verily believe; I could lay my finger on some of them. That Madison does not mean it, I also verily believe; and I rather believe the same of Jefferson, but I read him upon the whole thus: "A man of profound ambition and violent passions."

You must be by this time tired of my epistle. Perhaps I have treated certain characters with too much severity. I have, however, not meant to do them injustice, and, from the bottom of my soul, believe I have drawn them truly; and it is of the utmost consequence to the public weal they should be viewed in their true colors. . . .

13 PRESIDENT WASHINGTON VOICES ALARM OVER DIVISIONS IN THE CABINET

In the summer of 1792 the differences between Hamilton and Jefferson were aired in a bitter newspaper duel between John Fenno's pro-Hamilton *Gazette of the United States* and Philip Freneau's pro-Jefferson *National Gazette*. Disturbed by the public controversy, the President expressed his concern in confidential letters to his two chief advisers. The language in the letter below to Jefferson, August 23, 1792, was closely followed in a letter to Hamilton, August 26, 1792. Fitzpatrick, ed., *Writings of George Washington*, XXXII, 130-31.

. . . How unfortunate, and how much is it to be regretted then, that whilst we are encompassed on all sides with avowed enemies and insidious friends, that internal dissensions should be harrowing and tearing our vitals. The last, to me, is the most serious, the most alarming, and the most afflicting of the two. And without more charity for the opinions and acts of one another in Governmental matters, or some more infallible criterion by which the truth of speculative opinions, before they have undergone the test of experience, are to be forejudged than has yet fallen to the lot of fallibility, I believe it will be difficult, if not impracticable, to manage the Reins of Government or to keep the parts of it together: for if, instead of laying our shoulders to the machine after measures are decided on, one pulls this way and another that, before the utility of the thing is fairly tried, it must, inevitably, be torn asunder. And, in my opinion the fairest prospect of happiness and prosperity that ever was presented to man, will be lost, perhaps for ever!

My earnest wish, and my fondest hope therefore is, that instead of wounding suspicions, and irritable charges, there may be liberal allowances, mutual forbearances, and temporising yieldings on *all sides*. Under the exercise of these, matters will go on smoothly, and, if possible, more prosperously. Without them every thing must rub; the Wheels of Government will clog; our enemies will triumph, and by throwing their weight into the disaffected Scale, may accomplish the ruin of the goodly fabric we have been erecting.

I do not mean to apply these observations, or this advice to any particular person, or character. I have given them in the same general terms to other Officers of the Government; because the disagreements which have arisen from difference of opinions, and the Attacks which have been made upon almost all the measures of government, and most of its Executive Officers, have, for a long time past, filled me with painful sensations; and cannot fail I think, of producing unhappy consequences at home and abroad.

14   JEFFERSON EXPLAINS HIS POSITION

Replying to the President's expression of concern over the Cabinet divisions, Jefferson discussed at length his differences with Hamilton, his position in regard to Hamiltonian measures, and his relationship with editor Philip Freneau. The letter, September 9, 1792, is Jefferson's best statement, contemporaneous with the dispute, of his differences with Hamilton. Ford, ed., *Writings of Thomas Jefferson*, VI, 101-9.

. . . I now take the liberty of proceeding to that part of your letter wherein you notice the internal dissentions which have taken place within our government, and their disagreeable effect on it's movements. That such dissentions have taken place is certain, and even among those who are nearest to you in the administration. To no one have they given deeper concern than myself; to no one equal mortification at being myself a part of them. Tho' I take to myself no more than my share of the general observations of your letter, yet I am so desirous ever that you should know the whole truth, and believe no more than the truth, that I am glad to seize every occasion of developing to you whatever I do or think relative to the government; and shall therefore ask permission to be more lengthy now than the occasion particularly calls for, or could otherwise perhaps justify.

When I embarked in the government, it was with a determination to intermeddle not at all with the legislature, and as little as possible with my co-departments. The first and only instance of variance from the former part of my resolution, I was duped into by the Secretary of the Treasury and made a tool for forwarding his schemes, not then sufficiently understood by me; and of all the errors of my political life, this has occasioned me the deepest regret. It has ever been my purpose to explain this to you, when, from being actors on the scene, we shall have become uninterested spectators only. The second part of my resolution has been religiously observed with the war department; and as to that of the Treasury, has never been farther swerved from than by the mere enunciation of my sentiments in conversation, and chiefly among those who, expressing the same sentiments, drew mine from me. If it has been supposed that I have ever intrigued among the members of the legislatures to defeat the plans of the Secretary of the Treasury, it is contrary to all truth. As I never had the desire to influence the members, so neither had I any other means than my friendships, which I valued too highly to risk by usurpations on their freedom of judgment, and the conscientious pursuit of their own sense of duty. That I have utterly, in my private conversations, disapproved of the system of the Secretary of the treasury, I acknowledge and avow: and this was not merely a speculative difference. His system flowed from principles adverse to liberty, and was calculated to undermine and demolish the republic, by creating an influence of his department over the members of the legislature. I saw this influence actually produced, and it's first fruits to be the establishment of the great outlines of his project by the votes of the very persons who, having swallowed his bait were laying themselves out to profit by his plans: and that had these persons withdrawn, as those interested in a question ever should, the vote of the disinterested majority was clearly the reverse of what they made it. These were no longer the votes then of the representatives of the people, but of deserters from the rights and interests of the people: and it was impossible to consider their decisions, which had nothing in view but to enrich themselves, as the measures of the fair majority, which ought always to be respected. If what was actually doing begat uneasiness in those who wished for virtuous government, what was further proposed was not less threatening to the friends of the Constitution. For, in a Report on the subject of manufactures (still to be acted on) it was expressly assumed that the general government has a right to exercise all powers which may be for the *general welfare,* that is to say, all the legitimate powers of government: since no government has a legitimate right to do what is not for the welfare of the governed. There was indeed a sham-limitation of the universality of this power *to cases where money is to be employed.* But about what is it that money cannot be employed? Thus the object of these plans taken together is to draw all the powers of government into the hands of the general legislature, to establish means for corrupting a sufficient corps in that legislature to divide the honest votes and preponderate, by their own, the scale which suited, and to have that corps under the command of the Secretary of the Treasury for the purpose of subverting step by step the principles of the constitution, which he has so often declared to be a thing of nothing which must be changed. Such views might have justified something more than mere expressions of dissent, beyond which, nevertheless, I never went. Has abstinence from the department committed to me been equally observed by him? To say nothing of other interferences equally known, in the case of the two nations with which we have the most intimate connections, France and England, my system was to give some satisfactory distinctions to the former, of little cost to us, in return for the solid advantages yielded us by them; and to have met the English with some restrictions which might induce them to abate their severities against our commerce. I have always supposed this coincided with your sentiments. Yet the Secretary of the treasury, by his cabals with members of the legislature, and by high-toned declamation on other occasions, has forced down his own system, which was exactly the reverse. He undertook, of his own authority, the conferences with the ministers of those two nations, and was, on every consultation, provided with some report of a conversation with the one or the other of them, adapted to his views. These views, thus made to prevail, their execution fell of course to me; and I can safely appeal to you, who have seen all my letters and proceedings, whether I have not carried them into execution as sincerely as if they had been my own, tho' I ever considered them as inconsistent with the honor and interest of our country. That they have been inconsistent with our interest is but too fatally proved by the stab to our navigation given by the French. So that if the question be By whose fault is it that Colonel Hamilton and myself have not drawn together? the answer will depend on that to two other questions; whose principles of administration best justify, by their purity, conscientious adherence? and which of us has, notwithstanding, stepped farthest into the controul of the department of the other?

To this justification of opinions, expressed in the way of conversation, against the views of Colonel Hamilton, I beg leave to add some notice of his late charges against me in Fenno's gazette; for neither the stile, matter, nor venom of the pieces alluded to can leave a doubt of their author. Spelling my name and character at full length to the public, while he conceals his own under the signature of "an American" he charges me 1. With having written letters from Europe to my friends to oppose the present constitution while depending. 2. With a desire of not paying the public debt. 3. With setting up a paper to decry and slander the government. 1. The first charge is most false. No man in the U. S. I suppose, approved of every title in the

constitution: no one, I believe approved more of it than I did: and more
of it was certainly disproved by my accuser than by me, and of it's parts
most vitally republican. Of this the few letters I wrote on the subject (not
half a dozen I believe) will be a proof: and for my own satisfaction and
justification, I must tax you with the reading of them when I return to
where they are. You will there see that my objection to the constitution was
that it wanted a bill of rights securing freedom of religion, freedom of the
press, freedom from standing armies, trial by jury, and a constant Habeas
corpus act. Colonel Hamilton's was that it wanted a king and house of
lords. The sense of America has approved my objection and added the bill
of rights, not the king and lords. I also thought a longer term of service,
insusceptible of renewal, would have made a President more independant.
My country has thought otherwise, and I have acquiesced implicitly. He
wishes the general government should have power to make laws binding the
states in all cases whatsoever. Our country has thought otherwise: has he
acquiesced? . . . 2. The second charge is equally untrue. My whole correspondence while in France, and every word, letter, and act on the subject
since my return, prove that no man is more ardently intent to see the public
debt soon and sacredly paid off than I am. This exactly marks the difference between Colonel Hamilton's views and mine, that I would wish the
debt paid tomorrow; he wishes it never to be paid, but always to be a thing
where with to corrupt and manage the legislature. 3. I have never enquired
what number of sons, relations and friends of Senators, representatives,
printers or other useful partisans Colonel Hamilton has provided for among
the hundred clerks of his department, the thousand excisemen, custom-
house officers, loan officers etc. etc. etc. appointed by him, or at his nod,
and spread over the Union; nor could ever have imagined that the man
who has the shuffling of millions backwards and forwards from paper into
money and money into paper, from Europe to America, and America to
Europe, the dealing out of Treasury-secrets among his friends in what time
and measure he pleases, and who never slips an occasion of making friends
with his means, that such an one I say would have brought forward a charge
against me for having appointed the poet Freneau translating clerk to my
office, with a salary of 250. dollars a year. That fact stands thus. While the
government was at New York I was applied to on behalf of Freneau to
know if there was any place within my department to which he could be
appointed. I answered there were but four clerkships, all of which I found
full, and continued without any change. When we removed to Philadelphia,
Mr. Pintard the translating clerk, did not chuse to remove with us. His
office then became vacant. I was again applied to there for Freneau, and
had no hesitation to promise the clerkship for him. I cannot recollect

whether it was at the same time, or afterwards, that I was told he had a thought of setting up a newspaper there. But whether then, or afterwards, I considered it as a circumstance of some value, as it might enable me to do, what I had long wished to have done, that is, to have the material parts of the Leyden gazette brought under your eye and that of the public, in order to possess yourself and them of a juster view of the affairs of Europe than could be obtained from any other public source. This I had ineffectually attempted through the press of Mr. Fenno while in New York, selecting and translating passages myself at first then having it done by Mr. Pintard the translating clerk, but they found their way too slowly into Mr. Fenno's papers. Mr. Bache essayed it for me in Philadelphia, but his being a daily paper, did not circulate sufficiently in the other states. He even tried, at my request, the plan of a weekly paper of recapitulation from his daily paper, in hopes that that might go into the other states, but in this too we failed. Freneau, as translating clerk, and the printer of a periodical paper likely to circulate thro' the states (uniting in one person the parts of Pintard and Fenno) revived my hopes that the thing could at length be effected. On the establishment of his paper therefore, I furnished him with the Leyden gazettes, with an expression of my wish that he could always translate and publish the material intelligence they contained; and have continued to furnish them from time to time, as regularly as I received them. But as to any other direction or indication of my wish how his press should be conducted, what sort of intelligence he should give, what essays encourage, I can protest in the presence of heaven, that I never did by myself or any other, directly or indirectly, say a syllable, nor attempt any kind of influence. I can further protest, in the same awful presence, that I never did by myself or any other, directly or indirectly, write, dictate or procure any one sentence or sentiment to be inserted *in his, or any other gazette,* to which my name was not affixed or that of my office. I surely need not except here a thing so foreign to the present subject as a little paragraph about our Algerine captives, which I put once into Fenno's paper. Freneau's proposition to publish a paper, having been about the time that the writings of Publicola, and the discourses on Davila had a good deal excited the public attention, I took for granted from Freneau's character, which had been marked as that of a good whig, that he would give free place to pieces written against the aristocratical and monarchical principles these papers had inculcated. This having been in my mind, it is likely enough I may have expressed it in conversation with others; tho' I do not recollect that I did. To Freneau I think I could not, because I had still seen him but once, and that was at a public table, at breakfast, at Mrs. Elsworth's, as I passed thro' New York the last year. And I can safely declare that my expectations

looked only to the chastisement of the aristocratical and monarchical writ-
ers, and not to any criticisms on the proceedings of government: Colonel
Hamilton can see no motive for any appointment but that of making a
convenient partizan. But you Sir, who have received from me recommendations of a Rittenhouse, Barlow, Paine, will believe that talents and science
are sufficient motives with me in appointments to which they are fitted:
and that Freneau, as a man of genius, might find a preference in my eye to
be a translating clerk, and make good title to the little aids I could give him
as the editor of a gazette, by procuring subscriptions to his paper, as I did
some, before it appeared, and as I have with pleasure done for the labours
of other men of genius. . . . As to the merits or demerits of his paper,
they certainly concern me not. He and Fenno are rivals for the public favor.
The one courts them by flattery, the other by censure, and I believe it will
be admitted that the one has been as servile, as the other severe. But is not
the dignity, and even decency of government committed, when one of it's
principal ministers enlists himself as an anonymous writer or paragraphist
for either the one or the other of them? No government ought to be without censors: and where the press is free, no one ever will. If virtuous, it
need not fear the fair operation of attack and defence. Nature has given to
man no other means of sifting out the truth either in religion, law, or politics. I think it as honorable to the government neither to know, nor notice,
it's sycophants or censors, as it would be undignified and criminal to pamper
the former and persecute the latter. . . .

. . . I confide that yourself are satisfied that, as to dissensions in the
newspapers, not a syllable of them has ever proceeded from me; and that
no cabals or intrigues of mine have produced those in the legislature, and
I hope I may promise, both to you and myself, that none will receive aliment
from me during the short space I have to remain in office. . . .

15   HAMILTON DEFENDS THE JAY TREATY

No issue served more to deepen party divisions in the 1790's than the
treaty negotiated with Great Britain in 1794 by John Jay. Senate
ratification in June 1795 was followed by an unsuccessful attempt of
House Republicans led by James Madison to block the treaty by refusing to appropriate funds to carry out its provisions. The most important
Federalist defense of the treaty was written by Hamilton and published
in a newspaper series under the name Camillus. From Number 1 (July
22, 1795), Lodge, ed., *Works of Alexander Hamilton*, V, 189-98.

It was to have been foreseen, that the treaty which Mr. Jay was
charged to negotiate with Great Britain, whenever it should appear, would

have to contend with many perverse dispositions and some honest prejudices; that there was no measure in which the government could engage,
so little likely to be viewed according to its intrinsic merits—so very likely
to encounter misconception, jealousy, and unreasonable dislike. For this,
many reasons may be assigned.

It is only to know the vanity and vindictiveness of human nature, to be
convinced, that while this generation lasts there will always exist among
us men irreconcilable to our present national Constitution; embittered in
their animosity in proportion to the success of its operations, and the disappointment of their inauspicious predictions. It is a material inference
from this, that such men will watch, with lynx's eyes, for opportunities of
discrediting the proceedings of the government, and will display a hostile
and malignant zeal upon every occasion, where they think there are any
prepossessions of the community to favor their enterprises. A treaty with
Great Britain was too fruitful an occasion not to call forth all their
activity. . . .

It was known, that the resentment produced by our revolution war with
Great Britain had never been entirely extinguished, and that recent injuries
had rekindled the flame with additional violence. It was a natural consequence of this, that many should be disinclined to any amicable arrangement with Great Britain, and that many others should be prepared to
acquiesce only in a treaty which should present advantages of so striking
and preponderant a kind as it was not reasonable to expect could be obtained, unless the United States were in a condition to give the law to Great
Britain, and as, if obtained under the coercion of such a situation, could
only have been the short-lived prelude of a speedy rupture to get rid of
them.

Unfortunately, too, the supposition of that situation has served to foster
exaggerated expectations; and the absurd delusion to this moment prevails,
notwithstanding the plain evidence to the contrary, which is deducible from
the high and haughty ground still maintained by Great Britain against
victorious France. . . .

To every man who is not an enemy to the national government, who is
not a prejudiced partisan, who is capable of comprehending the argument,
and dispassionate enough to attend to it with impartiality, I flatter myself
I shall be able to demonstrate satisfactorily in the course of some succeeding
papers:

1. That the treaty adjusts, in a reasonable manner, the points in controversy between the United States and Great Britain, as well those depending on the inexecution of the treaty of peace, as those growing out of the
present European war.

2. That it makes no improper concessions to Great Britain, no sacrifices on the part of the United States.

3. That it secures to the United States equivalents for what they grant.

4. That it lays upon them no restrictions which are incompatible with their honor or their interest.

5. That in the articles which respect war, it conforms to the laws of nations.

6. That it violates no treaty with, nor duty towards, any foreign power.

7. That, compared with our other commercial treaties, it is, upon the whole entitled to a preference.

8. That it contains concessions of advantages by Great Britain to the United States, which no other nation has obtained from the same power.

9. That it gives to her no superiority of advantages over other nations with whom we have treaties.

10. That the interests of primary importance to our general welfare are promoted by it.

11. That the too probable result of a refusal to ratify is war, or, what would be still worse, a disgraceful passiveness under violations of our rights, unredressed, and unadjusted; and consequently that it is the true interest of the United States that the treaty should go into effect.

16 THE KENTUCKY RESOLUTIONS
OF 1798 AND 1799

The alien and sedition laws enacted by the Federalist Congress under Adams became a major party issue. The strongest Republican protests, the preliminary drafts of which were secretly written by Jefferson and Madison, came from the legislatures of Kentucky and Virginia. The excerpts below are the opening resolution of the 1798 Kentucky Resolutions and the final resolution of the 1799 protest. Jonathan Elliot, ed., *The Debates in the Several State Conventions, on the Adoption of the Federal Constitution* . . . (second edition, Washington: 1836), IV, 566, 571-72.

I. RESOLVED, That the several States composing the United States of America, are not united on the principle of unlimited submission to their General Government; but that by compact under the style and title of a Constitution for the United States, and of amendments thereto, they constituted a General Government for special purposes, delegated to that government certain definite powers, reserving, each State to itself, the residuary mass of right to their own self-government; and, that whensoever the General Government assumes undelegated powers, its acts are unauthoritative, void, and of no force; that to this compact each State acceded as a State, and is an integral party; that this Government, created by this compact, was not made the exclusive or final judge of the extent of the powers delegated to itself, since that would have made its discretion, and not the Constitution, the measure of its powers; but, that as in all other cases of compact, among parties having no common judge, *each party has an equal right to judge for itself, as well of infractions as of the mode and measure of redress.*

Resolved, That this Commonwealth considers the Federal Union, upon the terms and for the purposes specified in the late compact, conducive to the liberty and happiness of the several States: That it does now unequivocally declare its attachment to the Union, and to that compact, agreeably to its obvious and real intention, and will be among the last to seek its dissolution: That if those who administer the General Government be permitted to transgress the limits fixed by that compact, by a total disregard to the special delegations of power therein contained, an annihilation of the State Governments, and the creation, upon their ruins, of a General Consolidated Government, will be the inevitable consequence: That the principle and construction, contended for by sundry of the state legislatures, that the General Government is the exclusive judge of the extent of the powers delegated to it, stop not short of *despotism*—since the discretion of those who administer the government, and not the *Constitution,* would be the measure of their powers: That the several states who formed that instrument being sovereign and independent, have the unquestionable right to judge of the infraction; and, *That a Nullification by those sovereignities, of all unauthorized acts done under color of that instrument is the rightful remedy:* That this Commonwealth does, under the most deliberate reconsideration, declare, that the said Alien and Sedition Laws are, in their opinion, palpable violations of the said Constitution; and, however cheerfully it may be disposed to surrender its opinion to a majority of its sister states, in matters of ordinary or doubtful policy, yet, in momentous regulations like the present, which so vitally wound the best rights of the citizen, it would consider a silent acquiescence as highly criminal: That although this commonwealth, as a party to the federal compact, will bow to the laws of the Union, yet, it does, at the same time, declare, that it will not now, or ever hereafter, cease to oppose, in a constitutional manner, every attempt, at what quarter soever offered, to violate that compact. And, finally, in order that no pretext or arguments may be drawn from a supposed acquiescence, on the part of this Commonwealth, in the constitutionality of those laws, and be thereby used as precedents for similar future violations of the Federal compact—this Commonwealth does now enter against them its solemn PROTEST.

17 RESOLUTIONS OF DINWIDDIE COUNTY, VIRGINIA, IN OPPOSITION TO THE MEASURES OF THE ADAMS ADMINISTRATION

These resolutions, adopted at a public meeting, November 19, 1798, offer one of the most comprehensive protests made by the Republican opposition and indicate clearly what Republicans considered to be major issues: the army, the navy, the diplomatic establishment, the national debt, and the alien and sedition laws. Richmond *Examiner,* December 6, 1798.

1. *Resolved as the opinion of this meeting,* That a militia composed of the body of the people, is the proper, natural and safe defence of a free state, and that regular armies, except in case of an invasion, or the certain prospect of an invasion, are not only highly detrimental to the public welfare, but dangerous to liberty:

Detrimental to the public welfare, because industrious men are heavily taxed to support those who do nothing; because indolence among the poor is publicly encouraged: the army being an asylum for all who do not choose to labour: because the young men who form the mass of an army, instead of being a drawback on the productive labor of the community, might be more beneficially employed in supporting by their industry themselves and their families, and paying their proportions of the public debt: because the same object, immediate defence against a sudden invasion, might be attained infinitely cheaper, by putting arms into the hands of every man capable of bearing them: and because, the spirit which leads to war, the curse and the disgrace of humanity, is greatly augmented by standing armies, to whose leaders it opens a prospect of greater wealth, and higher military honors: and

Dangerous to liberty, because when numerous, they have tyrannized, as the experience of all ages has proved, both over the people and the government, and when limited, have always been subservient to the views of the executive department, from which they derive their honors and emoluments: because these honors and emoluments furnish an ample fund, by means of which the executive is enabled to reward its partizans and increase the number of its adherents: because a people accustomed to look for protection from external violence, to a standing army, become abject, debased and gradually enslaved; but knowing themselves to be the only defenders of their country, soon acquire that discipline and courage, which insure safety not only from foreign enemies, but domestic tyrants; and because, military establishments are in their nature progressive, the vast expense attending them, producing discontent and disturbances, and these furnishing a pretext for providing a force still more formidable; thus finally occasioning the oppression, the ruin, the SLAVERY of the people.

2. *Resolved as the opinion of this meeting,* That the plan for establishing a great naval armament is impolitic and pernicious; because it enlarges still more the fund for increasing executive influence: because the expense is incalculable, and in fact cannot be supported by legitimate taxation: because this country cannot hope to protect its commerce by a fleet, as no other country has ever done so, or to guard from invasion a coast fifteen hundred miles in extent: because it will teach the people to look for protection, not in themselves, their patriotism, their union, and their courage; but in a system in which they will not find it; because if the people of the United States, following the councils of their late president, avoid all political connexions, with European powers, they may reasonably expect to be seldom involved in the calamities of war, and having, fortunately, no islands in the West Indies, or Mediterranean, to defend, or conquests in the east to maintain, their ships must perish in the intervals of peace, to be preserved at an expense no less monstrous than unnecessary: and because experience has proved that even in a country whose existence is admitted now to depend on a fleet, seamen cannot be obtained, but by impressments, incompatible with law, liberty and humanity.

When therefore the navy of the United States is competent to the protection, not of our extensive coast, nor of our commerce throughout the world, but of our sea ports and coasting trade, from privateering and piratical depredations, it has attained the point, beyond which it ought not to go: beyond which benefit is partial, trifling, and precarious, and expense insupportable.

3. *Resolved also, as the opinion of this meeting,* that the government of the United States ought not to form an alliance with any nation on earth; that the people of America are competent to their own defence; that they are decidedly opposed to the plan of being drawn into the "foul abominations" of European politics, by any alliance with any government whatever, conscious that they must pay full value for what they receive, besides being entangled in ruinous connexions.

They reprobate therefore the practice of maintaining ministers resident in foreign countries, in the extent to which it is carried by the executive of the United States; because it adds still more to the already enormous mass of presidential patronage; because every important political view might be accomplished by a single minister advantageously stationed, and every valuable commercial purpose might be effected under the ordinary consular establishments; and because at a time like this, when money is borrowed to supply the deficiency of the taxes, every expense not absolutely necessary ought to be avoided.

Under these impressions they condemn the mission of William Smith to Lisbon, and of John Quincy Adams to Berlin: because there is but little commerce with Portugal and none with Prussia. In both cases therefore, and especially the latter, unless some political connection between the two countries is contemplated, an event surely not to be apprehended, the office is a sinecure and the salary thrown away.

4. *Resolved also, as the opinion of this meeting,* that the only proper way to raise money for national purposes, is by taxes, duties, excises and imposts, and that the power of borrowing money, ought not to be exercised except in cases of absolute necessity; that if money be really wanted, the people ought to be taxed to pay it; if not wanted, it ought not to be raised; if the public exigencies are supplied in the way first mentioned, economy must be observed: the people feeling immediately the effect of every public measure, would see that no unnecessary expense was incurred, and the money raised was duly expended; that the latter plan increases executive influence, augments the public debt, without the direct knowledge of the people; creates a paper monied interest, always adverse to the general welfare, and thrown on posterity, a burthen, which must either ruin them by its weight, or be shaken off in the struggles of a revolution.

5. *Resolved also, as the opinion of this meeting,* that the alien bill passed at the last session of Congress, is unnecessary, repugnant to humanity, and contrary to the constitution: the first, because its warmest advocates though called on, could mention neither persons nor facts to justify it: the second because it subjects the natives of foreign countries, who have sought here an asylum from persecution, to the despotism of a single individual: and the last, because the punishment of exile is inflicted without a public accusation of the party in the presence of the witnesses, and a trial by jury, which the constitution of the United States solemnly guarantees to every member of the community.

6. *Resolved also, as the opinion of this meeting,* that the freedom of the press is the great bulwark of liberty and can never be restrained but by a despotic government.

The people here present, solemnly impressed with this momentous truth, regard with astonishment, regret and indignation, the act of congress passed at the last session, commonly called the Sedition Bill. They denounce it to their fellow citizens, as a daring and unconstitutional violation of a sacred and essential right, without which, liberty, political science, and national prosperity are at an end. . . .

18 JEFFERSON EXPOUNDS THE REPUBLICAN PURPOSE

As the election of 1800 approached, Jefferson in numerous letters explained the fundamental principles in which he believed and for which he felt the Republican party was striving. This excerpt from his letter to Elbridge Gerry, January 26, 1799, is the best statement of the basic platform upon which Jefferson sought the presidency. Ford, ed., *Writings of Thomas Jefferson*, VII, 327-29.

I do then, with sincere zeal, wish an inviolable preservation of our present federal constitution, according to the true sense in which it was adopted by the States, that in which it was advocated by it's friends, and not that which it's enemies apprehended, who therefore became it's enemies; and I am opposed to the monarchising it's features by the forms of it's administration, with a view to conciliate a first transition to a President and Senate for life, and from that to a hereditary tenure of these offices, and thus to worm out the elective principle. I am for preserving to the States the powers not yielded by them to the Union, and to the legislature of the Union it's constitutional share in the division of powers; and I am not for transferring all the powers of the States to the general government, and all those of that government to the Executive branch. I am for a government rigorously frugal and simple, applying all the possible savings of the public revenue to the discharge of the national debt; and not for a multiplication of officers and salaries merely to make partisans, and for increasing, by every device, the public debt, on the principle of it's being a public blessing. I am for relying, for internal defence, on our militia solely, till actual invasion, and for such a naval force only as may protect our coasts and harbors from such depredations as we have experienced; and not for a standing army in time of peace, which may overawe the public sentiment; nor for a navy, which, by it's own expenses and the eternal wars in which it will implicate us, will grind us with public burthens, and sink us under them. I am for free commerce with all nations; political connection with none; and little or no diplomatic establishment. And I am not for linking ourselves by new treaties with the quarrels of Europe; entering that field of slaughter to preserve their balance, or joining in the confederacy of kings to war against the principles of liberty. I am for freedom of religion, and against all maneuvres to bring about a legal ascendancy of one sect over another: for freedom of the press, and against all violations of the constitution to silence by force and not by reason the complaints or criticisms, just or unjust, of our citizens against the conduct of their agents. And I am for encouraging the progress of science in all it's branches; and not for raising a hue and cry against the sacred name of philosophy; for awing the human mind by stories of raw-head and bloody bones to a distrust of its own vision, and to repose implicitly on that of others; to go backwards instead of forwards to look for improvement; to believe that government, religion, morality, and every other science were in the highest perfection in ages of the darkest ignorance, and that nothing can ever be devised more perfect than what was established by our forefathers. To these I will add, that I was a sincere well-wisher to the success of the French revolution, and still wish it may end in the establishment of a free and well-ordered republic; but I have not been insensible under the atrocious depredations they have committed on our commerce. The first object of my heart is my own country. In that is embarked my family, my fortune, and my own existence. I have not one farthing of interest, nor one fibre of attachment out of it, nor a single motive of preference of any one nation to another, but in proportion as they are more or less friendly to us. But though deeply feeling the injuries of France, I did not think war the surest means of redressing them. I did believe, that a mission sincerely disposed to preserve peace, would obtain for us a peaceable and honorable settlement and retribution; and I appeal to you to say, whether this might not have been obtained, if either of your colleagues had been of the same sentiment with yourself.

These, my friend, are my principles; they are unquestionably the principles of the great body of our fellow citizens, and I know there is not one of them which is not yours also. In truth, we never differed but on one ground, the funding system; and as, from the moment of it's being adopted by the constituted authorities, I became religiously principled in the sacred discharge of it to the uttermost farthing, we are united now even on that single ground of difference.

19 JEFFERSON'S FIRST INAUGURAL ADDRESS

Jefferson's address of March 4, 1801, is the finest contemporary summary of the ideology of Jeffersonian democracy. Its contents had clearly been foreshadowed by such campaign statements as that above. Andrew A. Lipscomb and Albert E. Bergh, eds., *The Writings of Thomas Jefferson* (Washington: 1903), III, 317-23.

During the contest of opinion through which we have passed, the animation of discussion and of exertions has sometimes worn an aspect which might impose on strangers unused to think freely and to speak and to write what they think; but this being now decided by the voice of the nation, announced according to the rules of the constitution, all will, of course, arrange themselves under the will of the law, and unite in common efforts for the common good. All, too, will bear in mind this sacred principle, that though the will of the majority is in all cases to prevail, that will, to be rightful, must be reasonable; that the minority possesses their equal rights, which equal laws must protect, and to violate which would be oppression. Let us, then, fellow citizens, unite with one heart and one mind. Let us restore to social intercourse that harmony and affection without which liberty and even life itself are but dreary things. And let us reflect that having banished from our land that religious intolerance under which mankind so long bled and suffered, we have yet gained little if we countenance a political intolerance as despotic, as wicked, and capable of as bitter and bloody persecutions. During the throes and convulsions of the ancient world, during the agonizing spasms of infuriated man, seeking through blood and slaughter his long-lost liberty, it was not wonderful that the agitation of the billows should reach even this distant and peaceful shore; that this should be more felt and feared by some and less by others; that this should divide opinions as to measures of safety. But every difference of opinion is not a difference of principle. We have called by different names brethren of the same principle. We are all republicans—we are all federalists. If there be any among us who would wish to dissolve this Union or to change its republican form, let them stand undisturbed as monuments of the safety with which error of opinion may be tolerated where reason is left free to combat it. I know, indeed, that some honest men fear that a republican government cannot be strong; that this government is not strong enough. But would the honest patriot, in the full tide of successful experiment, abandon a government which has so far kept us free and firm, on the theoretic and visionary fear that this government, the world's best hope, may by possibility want energy to preserve itself? I trust not. I believe this, on the contrary, the strongest government on earth. I believe it the only one where every man, at the call of the laws, would fly to the standard of the law, and would meet invasions of the public order as his own personal concern. Sometimes it is said that man can not be trusted with the government of himself. Can he, then, be trusted with the government of others? Or have we found angels in the forms of kings to govern him? Let history answer this question.

Let us, then, with courage and confidence pursue our own federal and republican principles, our attachment to our union and representative government. Kindly separated by nature and a wide ocean from the exterminating havoc of one quarter of the globe; too high-minded to endure the degradations of the others; possessing a chosen country, with room enough for our descendants to the hundredth and thousandth generation; entertaining a due sense of our equal right to the use of our own faculties, to the acquisitions of our industry, to honor and confidence from our fellow citizens, resulting not from birth but from our actions and their sense of them; enlightened by a benign religion, professed, indeed, and practiced in various forms, yet all of them including honesty, truth, temperance, gratitude, and the love of man; acknowledging and adoring an overruling Providence, which by all its dispensations proves that it delights in the happiness of man here and his greater happiness hereafter; with all these blessings, what more is necessary to make us a happy and prosperous people? Still one thing more, fellow citizens—a wise and frugal government, which shall restrain men from injurying one another, which shall leave them otherwise free to regulate their own pursuits of industry and improvement, and shall not take from the mouth of labor the bread it has earned. This is the sum of good government, and this is necessary to close the circle of our felicities.

About to enter, fellow citizens, on the exercise of duties which comprehend everything dear and valuable to you, it is proper that you should understand what I deem the essential principles of our government, and consequently those which ought to shape its administration. I will compress them within the narrowest compass they will bear, stating the general principle, but not all its limitations. Equal and exact justice to all men, of whatever state or persuasion, religious or political; peace, commerce, and honest friendship, with all nations—entangling alliances with none; the support of the state governments in all their rights, as the most competent administrations for our domestic concerns and the surest bulwarks against anti-republican tendencies; the preservation of the general government in its whole constitutional vigor, as the sheet anchor of our peace at home and safety abroad; a jealous care of the right of election by the people—a mild and safe corrective of abuses which are lopped by the sword of revolution where peaceable remedies are unprovided; absolute acquiescence in the decisions of the majority—the vital principle of republics, from which is no appeal but to force, the vital principle and immediate parent of despotism; a well-disciplined militia—our best reliance in peace and for the first moments of war, till regulars may relieve them; the supremacy of the civil over the military authority; economy in the public expense, that labor may be lightly burthened; the honest payment of our debts and sacred preservation of the public faith; encouragement of agriculture, and of commerce as its handmaid; the diffusion of information and arraignment of all abuses at the bar of the public reason; freedom of religion; freedom of the press, and freedom of person under the protection of the *habeas corpus;* and trial by juries impartially selected—these principles form the bright constellation which has gone before us, and guided our steps through an age of revolution and reformation. The wisdom of our sages and blood of our heroes have been devoted to their attainment. They should be the creed of our political faith—the text of civic instruction—the touchstone by which to try the services of those we trust; and should we wander from them in moments of error or alarm, let us hasten to retrace our steps and to regain the road which alone leads to peace, liberty, and safety.

20   ROBERT GOODLOE HARPER SPEAKS
FOR THE FEDERALISTS

A South Carolina Federalist who had served in Congress since 1795, Harper was defeated for re-election in the Republican victory of 1800. In a farewell circular letter to his constituents, March 5, 1801, Harper reviewed at length the years of Federalist power and reflected on the maxims of his party. Broadside in Albert Gallatin Papers, New-York Historical Society.

The leading principle of their [Federalist] system, as to foreign nations, has been, to preserve peace and amity with all, by a conduct just liberal and fair towards all; but to grant particular privileges to none, and to submit to indignities from none: to rely, for the protection of our rights and honor, not on the friendship the justice or the forbearance of other governments, but on our own strength and resources; and to employ vigorous means for calling forth those resources, and preparing them for exertion in time of need: in fine, to hold the olive branch in one hand, and the sword in the other; to employ peaceable means for attaining our just objects, while peaceable means could afford rational hopes of success; and to shew ourselves ready to resort to force, should those hopes be found fallacious.

Regulating its conduct by these maxims, the government of the United States, under the direction of the federalists, with Washington and afterwards Adams at their head, has preserved the nation in peace, through the most general and most furious war, that has afflicted the world in modern times. To understand fully the difficulties of this task, it must be recollected, that the war raged with great violence in the West-Indies, where we carry on a most extensive commerce; and that the chief parties in it, both there and in Europe, were France and England, the two greatest trading and maritime powers in the world, and those with which we had the most extensive connections, both commercial and political: one perpetually demanding what could not be granted without exciting the jealousy, and perhaps infringing the rights, of the other; each endeavouring to draw us, by indirect means, into the quarrel; one in order to make use of us, and the other to plunder us; and each committing, from time to time, aggressions on our trade, which our honour and our interest forbad us to submit to, their pride and resentment prevented them from atoning for, and perhaps their policy withheld them from restraining.

Between these two dangerous shoals, the vessel of the state has been safely steered, by its federal pilots. . . .

In the management of our domestic affairs, their system has been, in the first to support vigourously the independence and authority of the federal government; which alone is capable of ensuring our safety from abroad, by opposing to foreign nations the barrier of our united strength; and of maintaining our peace at home, by checking the ambition and repressing the passions of the several states, and balancing their forces so as to prevent the greater from overpowering and subduing the lesser. They well knew that this government, being under the necessity of laying and collecting considerable taxes, of raising and supporting armies and fleets, of maintaining numerous officers, and of carrying on all those expensive operations which its superintendance of our general affairs require, and from which the state governments are wholly exempt, is far more likely than those governments to incur unpopularity, to become subject to the imputation of extravagance oppression and ambitious views, and to be deprived of the public confidence. They well knew that this government, being removed at a greater distance than the state governments from the people, was more apt to be viewed with jealousy, and considered as a foreign government; and that there never would be wanting ambitious and restless men, who failing to obtain that share of influence in the federal government, or those honours and employments under it, to which they might think themselves entitled, would take refuge in the state governments, and avail themselves of all those circumstances to render the federal government odious, to excite against it the public resentment, and even to over-rule and controul it by means of the state governments. Well knowing this, the federalists considered it as a principle of the utmost importance, for the preservation of the federal government, to render it as independent as possible of state influence, to give it a movement of its own, and complete power to enforce its own laws; to resist state encroachments; and to restrain the state governments within their just and proper bounds. In every struggle between the federal and the state governments, they considered the latter as possessing infinitely the greatest natural strength; and therefore thought it their duty, to take part with the former, in order to preserve the balance.

As to the federal government itself, their second great maxim was, to support the executive power, against the encroachments, the ambition, and the superior strength of the popular branch. The power of a popular assembly, being little suspected by the people, is always little watched; and no one member is to bear the blame of any excesses which the whole body may commit, its power is but little restrained by personal responsibility and a regard to character; and of course is very likely to be abused. Hence has resulted, in every age and nation where the form of government admitted popular assemblies, a constant effort, on the part of those assemblies, to get all power into their own hands, and to exercise it according to their own passions and caprice. This has every where produced the necessity of checking the power of those assemblies, by confining it wholly to legislation, by dividing that power between two houses, and by giving the judicial and executive powers to persons independent of the legislature. This has been done by our constitution; which gives the executive power to the President, a single magistrate; places the judicial power in the courts; and divides the legislative power between the Senate and House of Representatives. This House of Representatives, being the most numerous and the most popular body, is subject to the same passions and dispositions which popular bodies ever feel; and, consequently, has a perpetual tendency to encroach on the executive powers, and to direct and controul the President in the exercise of his authority. As the President, being a single magistrate, is much more apt to be suspected and viewed with a jealous eye, than this popular assembly, which the people consider as nearer to themselves and more under their controul, he would have the people against him in these contests, and must finally submit absolutely to the controul of the House, were there not always some members of it, whose just way of thinking and regard to the constitution induce them to oppose the improper enterprizes of their own body, and defend the executive power against its perpetual attacks. This was the conduct of the federalists. Knowing the executive power to be absolutely essential for preserving the due balance of the constitution, and for conducting the affairs of the nation with prudence steadiness and success; and knowing it also to be, in itself, much weaker than its antagonist; they made themselves its defenders, and by their perseverance and talents have thus far succeeded, in preserving to it the weight and authority designed for it by the constitution. . . .

Thus far of the principles of government itself. As to the administration of the government, the federalists laid it down as the corner stone of their system, to support cherish and invigorate commerce, as the best and indeed the only effectual means, of promoting agriculture, and every other branch of industry. Commerce is as necessary to the farmer as rain or manure. Commerce supplies markets; and every farmer knows that the more and better markets there are, the higher he can sell his produce, and the cheaper he can purchase his goods, the more agriculture will flourish and the country thrive. The more ships and merchants we have, the more buyers will there be for our crops, and the better price we shall get. Ships and commerce make large towns, and the more large towns we have, the more demand there will be for provisions, and the higher will be their price. Increase the market and the demand, and you increase the price of produce and the profits of labour; and with them the general industry and prosperity of the country. . . .

Surely that branch of industry which so greatly promotes all the rest, and furnishes besides almost the whole of our revenue, deserves the fostering care of government. To estimate rightly the importance of commerce, we must consider what our condition would be, if we were deprived of markets for the sale of our produce, and called on, at the same time, for a direct tax of six or seven millions of dollars. How should we find money to pay it?

It is equally important in another point of view. A large and most important part of our country, depends on commerce wholly for its wealth, and in a great degree for its subsistence. I speak of the eastern states, which constitute one third of the union. A vast portion of their property consists in ships; and great numbers of their people are merchants or sailors. Should the protection of the government be withheld from commerce, these people would be deprived, almost entirely, of all benefit from the union; and it cannot be conceived that they would long live under a government, by which their interests should be sacrificed or neglected, in a point so essential.

Various measures were adopted by the federalists, for the encouragement of commerce; among which were the establishment and encouragement of banks; the encouragement of insurance offices; the institution of equal and permanent regulations respecting trade; the allowance of drawbacks; the establishment of an uniform system of bankruptcy; the formation of commercial treaties with foreign nations; the sending of ministers and consuls into the various commercial countries of Europe, for watching over our commercial interests, and protecting and assisting our trading citizens; the erection of light-houses; the fortification of ports; and some others of less moment: but the great and efficacious measure, without which all the others would have been unavailing, was the establishment of a naval force for the protection of our trade at sea. The true and only method of promoting industry, is to protect property, and secure to every man the fruit of his labour. As no farmer would raise a crop, if his neighbour, being stronger than him, might come and take it from him; so no merchant will build a ship, or purchase a cargo, to send to sea, if it is exposed to the grasp of every plunderer. It was therefore a leading object in the system of the federalists, to establish a navy. Their exertions in this respect have been too much embarrassed and impeded, by the constant opposition of the other party, to be carried as far as they ought to have gone; but under all the difficulties thrown in their way, they have produced most important and beneficial effects.

III THE PARTY MANAGERS

The leadership essential to success in any political structure appears to have been even more significant in the early phases of party development, when formal organization and machinery were rudimentary and party procedures had not become firmly established. While their activities were regarded with suspicion by many, party managers initiated new techniques of marshaling public support, nominating candidates, placing their programs before the voters, getting out the vote on election days, and maintaining unity among party supporters. Some of the most successful of these early party managers, such as John Beckley, clerk of the House of Representatives, were not often in the public spotlight; others, such as Alexander Hamilton or Aaron Burr, were usually in the thick of public controversy. Members of Congress were important figures in the management of both the Federalist and the Republican parties and clearly demonstrated this influence in the congressional nominating caucuses. Madison, as leader of the Republican party in Congress until 1797, and Jefferson, after 1797, as Vice-President and active head of the Republican party, assisted local party managers. As President, Jefferson recognized the importance of maintaining effective party leadership both in Congress and in the states. The confidential communications between early party leaders offer revealing insights into the operation of parties and provide behind-the-scenes information of a type rarely found after the invention of the telephone.

21   JAMES MADISON ORGANIZES
THE ADOPTION OF PUBLIC RESOLUTIONS

Resolutions regarding relations with France and the conduct of French
Minister Edmond Charles Genet were adopted at several public meetings in Virginia in September, 1793, expressing the position that Madison outlines below. How these resolutions came to be adopted is also
explained. John Taylor of Caroline, whom Madison had asked to help
in arranging meetings, comments on the success of the plans. Hunt,
ed., *Writings of James Madison*, VI, 188-93; *John P. Branch Historical
Papers of Randolph-Macon College*, II (1905-8), 259-60.

Madison to Archibald Stuart
   September 1, 1793

Being well persuaded of your attachment to the public good, I make
no apology for mentioning to you a few circumstances which I conceive
to be deeply connected with it. It appears by accounts received by Col.
[James] Monroe and myself from Mr. Jefferson, as well as by the face of
the late Newspapers that a variance of a very serious nature has taken
place between the federal executive and Mr. Genet the French Minister.
From whatever causes it may have particularly resulted, and whatever
blame may belong to the latter, the event will give great pain to all those
enlightened friends of those principles of liberty on which the American
and French Revolutions are founded, and of that sound policy which ought
to maintain the connection between the two countries. Unfortunately this
character is not due to every description of person among us. There are some
who dislike Republican Government. There are others who dislike the connection with France. And there are others misled by the influence of both.
From these quarters attempts are already issuing to make the worst instead
of the best of the event, to turn the public . . . in respect to Genet against
the French Nation, to give the same turn to the public veneration for the
President to produce by these means an animosity between America and
France, as the hopeful source of the dissolution of their political and commercial union, of a consequent connection with Great Britain and under her auspices to a gradual approximation to her Form of Government. In this state of
things is it not the duty of all good citizens to deliberate on the best steps that
can be taken for defecting the mischief? And can there be any doubt that a
true and authentic expression of the sense of the people will be the most
effectual as well as the most proper antidote that can be applied? It is as

little doubtful in my opinion what the sense of the people is. They are attached by the Constitution. They are attached to the President. They are attached to the French Nation and Revolution. They are attached to peace as long as it can be honorably preserved. They are averse to Monarchy and to a political connection with that of Great Britain and will readily protest against any known or supposed danger that may have this change in their situation for their object. Why then cannot the sense of the people be collected on these points by the agency of temperate and respectable men who have the opportunity of meeting them. This is the more requisite in the country at large at present as the voice of particular plans distinguished by particular interests and opinions may otherwise be mistaken as that of the nation and every hope be thence cut off of preserving the esteem and affection as yet existing between the French and the American people. A great deal might be said on this subject: To you a very little will suffice and the less as you will learn from Col. Monroe all the particulars which may explain the ground of what I have taken the liberty of suggesting. I shall only therefore add my request that you consider this letter as entirely confidential. . . .

Madison to Jefferson
September 2, 1793

. . . It is . . . of such infinite importance to our own Government as well as to that of France, that the real sentiments of the people here should be understood, that something ought to be attempted on that head. I inclose a copy of a train of Ideas sketched on the first rumour of the war between the Executive and Genet, and particularly suggested by the Richmond Resolutions, as a groundwork for those who might take the lead in County meetings. It was intended that they should be modified in every particular according to the state of information and the particular temper of the place. A copy has been sent to Caroline with a hope that Mr. [Edmund] P[endleton] might find it not improper to step forward. Another is gone to the District Court at Staunton in the hands of Monroe, who carried a letter from me on the subject to A[rchibald] Stuart; and a third will be for consideration at the District Court at Charlottesville. If these examples should be set, there may be a chance of like proceedings elsewhere; and in themselves they will be respectable specimens of the principles and sensations of the Agricultural which is the commanding part of the Society. . . .

Taylor to Madison
  September 25, 1793

Instantly on receipt of yours from Albemarle, notifications were dispersed, and in five days, resolutions were formed by a very numerous
meeting. They are in some papers, and will appear in others. I hope you
will approve of them. I wish they may differ enough . . . to avoid a
suspicion of their being coined in the same mint. I was obliged to come
forward in a specification. But, as I thought best, the chairman fathered
and conducted, the whole business.

22   A CAMPAIGN MANAGER IN ACTION

John Beckley, clerk of the United States House of Representatives,
was one of the most active Republican managers of the 1790's. Operating from the national capital in Philadelphia, he managed the 1796
Jeffersonian presidential campaign in Pennsylvania with a professional
skill rarely equaled at the time and delivered 14 of the state's 15 electoral votes to Jefferson. The techniques that Beckley employed are
illustrated in a series of letters written during the course of the campaign to General William Irvine, an influential political leader in
central Pennsylvania. Additional details concerning Republican activities in 1796 are supplied in Beckley's letter supporting the successful
application of John Smith of Philadelphia for appointment as federal
marshal of eastern Pennsylvania in 1801—one of President Jefferson's
earliest appointments. Beckley's letters to Irvine are in the Historical
Society of Pennsylvania; the recommendation of Smith is in the Appointment Papers: Applications and Recommendations, 1801-9, National Archives.

John Beckley to William Irvine
  Philadelphia, 15th September 1796

. . . The president has at last concluded to decline a reelection, and has
forwarded on to the Governor of each state a notification thereof, to be
published in each state at the same time, so that we may expect to see it
published here about the 1st of next month. You will readily perceive that
this short Notice is designed to prevent a fair Election, and the consequent
choice of Mr. Jefferson. It will not however produce that effect, if your
state make but a reasonable exertion—the general sentiment is in favor
of Jefferson, and I think a little exertion by a few good active republicans in
each *County* would bring the people out, and defeat the influence of your
little rotten towns such as Carlisle, Lancaster, York, etc. A silent, but

certain cooperation among the country people may do much. In my next I will send you a list of the republican Electors, that have been agreed upon for this State, and hope you will be able to scatter a few copies thro' *some proper hands*. It will not be forgotten that no ticket must be printed. From Georgia, North Carolina, South Carolina, Virginia, Kentucky and Tennessee we expect a unanimous vote—half Maryland and Delaware—some in New Jersey, and several to the Eastward—so that if Pennsylvania do well the Election is safe. In the City and County [of Philadelphia] we expect to carry the republican ticket by a large Majority. Have you any western friends that you can drop a line to, to assist us? What seems to be the sentiment, if any, in the Country you passed thro'? Cannot an effectual exertion be made? It is now or never for the republican cause. . . .

Philadelphia, 22nd September 1796

. . . By this mail you will receive the presidents address of declension to serve again, and I enclose you a list of the Electors agreed to here, just before the Assembly adjourned. Governor Mifflins name being added in the room of Mr. Rittenhouse, deceased; the Governor is as fully eligible as Judge McKean, and it is believed his name will greatly assist the ticket. I shall decline, until I have the pleasure to see you, any remarks on the presidents address, and only say that we have every assurance of success in favor of Mr. Jefferson to the Southward. How it will be to the Eastward I am not yet informed. Your state must decide it, and I hope every exertion will be made. A few Copies of the lists of the Electors, with the names plainly written, dispersed in a few judicious hands in the Country, and copies of them scattered about in different neighbourhoods, would do great good, if the people are warned of the day, and a few popular men will endeavor to bring them out. By next post I will endeavor to send you some handbills, by way of address to the people of Pennsylvania, shewing the strong reasons there is for this States having a Southern, rather than an Eastern president. . . .

P.S. The Governor declines being put on the ticket of Electors—no name is yet concluded on in his room; it will be either Charles Biddle, or Thomas Barclay—tomorrow it will be decided and by Tuesdays mail I will inform you.

Philadelphia, 30th September 1796

I enclose you a complete list of the ticket for Electors, and by next mail, or before, I will forward you a dozen or two hand bills on the same subject.

By every information we can get Mr. Jefferson will have a unanimous Vote in every Southern State, except Maryland, and there about half. To the Eastward of the North river, we count certain on Eight votes, perhaps more. Rhode Island will be with us—two in New Hampshire—three or 4 in Massachusetts, and one or two in Vermont and Connecticut. If Pennsylvania stirs, the business is safe. . . .

Philadelphia, 4th October 1796

. . . Inclosed are 6 copies of an address to the people of Pennsylvania —by next mail on Friday, or by first *certain* opportunity, will forward you 100 more. It would be most advisable however to push them on over the Mountain, before they are circulated below, which will prevent any counter address. 1000 Copies are struck and will be dispersed in such manner that they may appear first above, before they come back to the City. Mr. Jefferson, has explicitly declared that if elected he will serve, and Mr. Patrick Henry, of Virginia, has as explicitly declared, that he neither wishes nor would accept the office. I am this moment advised by a letter from New York, that Mr. Hamilton publickly declares, that he thinks it would be best on the score of conciliation and expediency to elect Mr. Jefferson, president, since he is the only man in America that could secure us the affections of the French republic. Will it not be advisable to throw this paragraph into the Carlisle paper?

It is too late now to make a change in the Electors—the Aristocrats say themselves that the Republican ticket is by far the best, and believe it will carry. Many of them prefer Pin[c]kney to Adams, and there will be great schism amongst them. Our accounts South and East, look well, and we have great hopes in New Jersey. . . .

Philadelphia, 17th October 1796

By old Doctor Nesbit, I have forwarded to you a packet with hand bills, which I must tax your goodness to put under way for the Western Country, so as to reach it before the Election for Electors. You best know what characters to address them to. In a few days a select republican friend from the City, will call upon you with a parcel of tickets to be distributed in your County. Any assistance and advice you can furnish him with, as to suitable districts and characters, will I am sure be rendered. He is one of two republican friends, who have undertaken to ride thro' all the middle and lower counties on this business, and bring with them 6 or 8 thousand tickets. It is necessary at the same time to aid the common object by getting all our friends to write as many tickets as they can, in their respective families, before the Elections. . . .

I enclose you a few copies of the ticket to disperse among such good friends, as will exert themselves, to get as many copies before the Election, as they can. . . .

Philadelphia, 2d November 1796

. . . We are all busily engaged in the Election, and are sanguine in our hopes of success for Jefferson. The other side are equally active and equally sanguine. I think however that including the City and County of Philadelphia, we shall carry a Majority for the Jefferson ticket. We hope the Counties below the Mountains will be nearly divided and that the Western Counties will carry the Election for us. I send you a copy of the last Address of the Republicans to the people. . . .

John Beckley's Recommendation of John Smith of Philadelphia
Philadelphia, 10th March 1801

Major John Smith, of this City, and myself were in the Year 1796, Members of the General Committee of the State of Pennsylvania appointed to promote the Election of Republican Electors for this State, of a president and Vice president of the United States. A special day of Election was appointed by law, of which, by the management of our political opponents, the people were kept in universal ignorance until a very late day, and, no State Elections being called for, rendered the people still more listless and indifferent;—added to which, the law itself required a very short previous promulgation by Officers almost wholly Federal, and it also demanded of every Voter a *Written* ticket with the names of the 15 Electors. Under these discouragements the Committee commenced its operations.—They caused copies of the law, notices of the day and manner of Election, suitable addresses, circular letters and *50,000 written tickets,* to be prepared and distributed thro' every County of the State.—11 Clerks were constantly employed—a Sub Committee of five of which the Subscriber was one, was established with permanent sittings—Expresses were dispatched in every direction, and finally Major Smith, whose known influence and general knowledge of all the principal Republican Characters in the State, rendered his services extremely desirable, voluntarily offered his services to the Committee, to take a tour thro' all the principal Counties below the Alleghany Mountains, and personally animate the people to action—they were accepted, and Major Smith accordingly, at his own expense, employed

25 days immediately preceeding the Election, and traversed the State in
various directions, thro' a journey of 7 or 800 miles, with the loss of a
very valuable horse killed by fatigue, and with a zeal, activity, intelligence
and exertion, seldom equalled, but never exceeded. To these exertions all
of which were fully and intimately known to me, I have always believed
and must ever believe, the success of that Election was principally, if not
altogether produced. . . .

23 ALEXANDER HAMILTON ATTEMPTS TO
ENLIST THE FORMER PRESIDENT'S PRESTIGE
IN THE FEDERALIST CAUSE

The most enterprising of Federalist leaders, Hamilton saw the tremen-
dous popular advantage of having Washington associated in the public
mind with the Federalist party and here, May 19, 1798, seeks to
draw the former President out of retirement. Although Washington
did not undertake the tour that Hamilton suggested, he accepted the
command of the army, with Hamilton as his second in command.
Lodge, ed., *Works of Alexander Hamilton*, X, 284-85.

At the present dangerous crisis of public affairs, I make no apology
for troubling you with a political letter. Your impressions of our situation,
I am persuaded, are not different from mine. There is certainly great probability that we may have to enter into a very serious struggle with France;
and it is more and more evident that the powerful faction which has for
years opposed the government, is determined to go every length with
France. I am sincere in declaring my full conviction, as the result of a long
course of observation, that they are ready to *new-model* our Constitution
under the *influence* or *coercion* of France, to form with her a perpetual
alliance, *offensive* and *defensive,* and to give her a monopoly of our trade
by *peculiar* and *exclusive* privileges. This would be in substance, whatever
it might be in name, to make this country a province of France. Neither
do I doubt that her standard, displayed in this country, would be directly
or indirectly seconded by them, in pursuance of the project I have mentioned.

It is painful and alarming to remark, that the opposition faction assumes
so much a geographical complexion. As yet, from the south of Maryland
nothing has been heard but accounts of disapprobation of our government,
and approbation of or apology for France. This is a most portentous symp-
tom, and demands every human effort to change it.

In such a state of public affairs, it is impossible not to look up to you,
and to wish that your influence could in some proper mode be brought into

direct action. Among the ideas which have passed through my mind for this purpose, I have asked myself whether it might not be expedient for you to make a circuit through Virginia and North Carolina, under some pretence of health, etc. This would call forth addresses, public dinners, etc., which would give you an opportunity of expressing sentiments in answers, toasts, etc., which would throw the weight of your character into the scale of the government, and revive an enthusiasm for your person, that may be turned into the right channel.

I am aware that the step is delicate, and ought to be well considered before it is taken. I have even not settled my own opinion as to its propriety, but I have concluded to bring the general idea under your view, confident that your judgment will make a right choice; and that you will take no step which is not well calculated. The conjuncture, however, is extraordinary, and now, or very soon, will demand extraordinary measures.

You ought also to be aware, my dear sir, that in the event of an open rupture with France, the public voice will again call you to command the armies of your country; and, though all who are attached to you will, from attachment, as well as from public considerations, deplore an occasion which should once more tear you from that repose to which you have so good a right, yet it is the opinion of all those with whom I converse, that you will be compelled to make the sacrifice. All your past labor may demand to give it efficacy this further, this very great sacrifice.

24 THOMAS JEFFERSON ASSISTS
REPUBLICAN ELECTIONEERING

Political customs did not yet embrace open campaigning by presidential candidates, but through friends, party lieutenants, and private correspondence, presidential candidates did assist in campaign activities. During the campaign of 1800, Jefferson expounded his views in private letters to influential persons who could be expected to make them known in their neighborhoods. He also arranged for the distribution of a number of political pamphlets, as indicated in the following excerpts from letters to Archibald Stuart, an influential Virginia Republican, and to Philip Norborne Nicholas, chairman of the Virginia Republican central committee. Ford, ed., *Writings of Thomas Jefferson*, VII, 354, 439.

Jefferson to Stuart
  February 13, 1799

. . . The materials now bearing on the public mind will infallibly restore it to it's republican soundness in the course of the present summer, if the knowledge of facts can only be disseminated among the people. Under separate cover you will receive some pamphlets written by George Nicholas on the acts of the last session. These I wish you to distribute, not to sound men who have no occasion for them, but to such as have been misled, are candid and will be open to the conviction of truth, and are of influence among their neighbors. It is the sick who need medicine, and not the well. Do not let my name appear in the matter. Perhaps I shall forward you some other things to be distributed in the same way. . . .

Jefferson to Nicholas
  April 7, 1800

Your favor of Feb. 2. came to hand Feb. 11. and I put off the acknowledging it, till I could forward to you some pamphlets on a subject very interesting to all the states, and containing views which I am anxious should be generally exhibited. In a former collection of tracts published by Mr. [Thomas] Cooper were two papers on Political arithmetic. He was printing a 2d edition of the whole, and was prevailed on to strike off an extra number of the two on Political arithmetic, adding to it some principles of government from a former work of his. I have forwarded to you by a vessel going from hence to Richmond 8. dozen of these, with a view that one should be sent to every county committee in the state, either from yourself personally or from your central committee. Tho' I know that this is not the immediate object of your institution, yet I consider it as a most valuable object, to which the institution may most usefully be applied. I trust yourself only with the secret that these pamphlets go from me. You will readily see what a handle would be made of my advocating their contents. I must leave to yourself therefore to say how they come to you. Very possibly they will have got to you before this does, as I shall retain it for a private conveyance and know of none as yet. I dare trust nothing this summer through the post offices. At other times they would not have such strong motives to infidelity. . . .

25 A NEW YORK REPUBLICAN EXPLAINS PARTY STRATEGY IN 1800

New York, which had voted for John Adams in 1796, was a key state in the presidential election of 1800. The selection of presidential electors by the legislature made the state election the crucial contest, and the party complexion of the legislature was likely to be determined by the delegation from New York City. There Aaron Burr concentrated the efforts of party management described by his close party lieutenant Matthew L. Davis to Albert Gallatin, March 29, 1800, a month prior to the Republican victory. Henry Adams, *The Life of Albert Gallatin* (Philadelphia: 1879), 233-34.

. . . Your opinion respecting the importance of our election for members of Assembly in this city is the prevailing opinion among our Republican friends. You ask, "What are your prospects?" All things considered, they are favorable. We have been so much deceived already that a prudent man perhaps will not hazard an opinion but with extreme diffidence. At the request of Mr. Nicholson, I shall briefly state the leading features of our plan. . . .

The Federalists have had a meeting and determined on their Senators; they have also appointed a committee to nominate suitable characters for the Assembly. Out of the thirteen that now represent the city, eleven decline standing again. They are much perplexed to find men. Mr. Hamilton is very busy, more so than usual, and no exertions will be wanting on his part. Fortunately, Mr. Hamilton will have at this election a most powerful opponent in Colonel Burr. This gentleman is extremely active; it is his opinion that the Republicans had better not publish a ticket or call a meeting until the Federalists have completed theirs. Mr. Burr is arranging matters in such a way as to bring into operation all the Republican interest. He is not to be on our nomination, but is to represent one of the country counties. At our first meeting he has pledged himself to come forward and address the people in firm and manly language on the importance of the election and the momentous crisis at which we have arrived. This he has never done at any former election, and I anticipate great advantages from the effect it will produce.

In addition to this, he has taken great trouble to ascertain what characters will be most likely to run well, and by his address has procured the assent of eleven or twelve of our most influential friends to stand as candidates. . . . On the whole, I believe we shall offer to our fellow-citizens the most formidable list ever offered them by any party in point of morality, public and private virtue, local and general influence, etc., etc. From this ticket and the exertions that indisputably will be made we have a right to expect much, and I trust we shall be triumphant. If we carry this election, it may be ascribed principally to Colonel Burr's management and perverance. Hamilton fears his influence; the party seem in a state of consternation, while ours possess more than usual spirits. Such are our prospects. We shall open the campaign under the most favorable impressions, and headed by a man whose intrigue and management is most astonishing. . . .

26 A NEW YORK FEDERALIST RELATES HIS EFFORTS IN THE ELECTION OF 1800

Something of the exertions of the Federalists in the New York City election is indicated by Robert Troup, one of Hamilton's closest friends, writing May 2, 1800, to Peter Van Schaack. *Van Schaak Papers, Library of Congress.*

I received your favor whilst I was much engaged with our court and since the court has adjourned I have been night and day employed in the business of the election. The polls closed last night and I believe, though we have not yet received accurate returns, that all the Democratic members of assembly have succeeded. As the seventh ward did not vote for our member of Congress but for the West Chester member we think it probable that our friend Col. Morton is elected. As to senators I can yet form no opinion. The election was extremely warm and contested. Never have I witnessed such exertions on either side before. I have not eaten dinner for three days and have been constantly upon my legs from 7 in the morning till 7 in the afternoon; and I am now not only worn out with fatigue but really sick. I consider the event of our election as fatal to the appointment of federal electors of President and vice-President and perhaps as fatal to our next election of Governor. I have a strong suspicion that we will not soon see a general exertion here on the part of the friends of the government; but that things will be suffered to take their course in the hands of the Jacobins. The burthen of opposition falls with too much inequality. The services well performed require a sacrifice of feeling which virtuous minds make with infinite difficulty—and the inevitable tendency of our system is to anarchy and ruin. The stratagems—the lies—the villainies we have had to contend with would astonish you!

27 A SOUTH CAROLINA REPUBLICAN REPORTS HIS ACTIVITIES IN THE CAMPAIGN OF 1800

Charles Pinckney, a United States Senator from South Carolina and a relative of Federalist vice-presidential candidate Charles Cotesworth Pinckney, managed the Jeffersonian campaign in South Carolina in 1800. Although Republicans lost in Charleston, Pinckney went to Columbia, where the legislature would select the presidential electors, and worked behind the scenes to carry the Jeffersonian slate. In the following reports to Jefferson, he recounts his efforts and supplies revealing information on Federalist activities. *American Historical Review,* IV (1898), 114-16, 118-19.

October 12: 1800

. . . The influence of the officers of the Government and of the Banks and of the British and Mercantile Interest will be very powerful in Charleston. I think we shall in the City as Usual loose two-thirds of the representation, but the City has generally not much influence at Columbia. Our Country Republican Interest has always been very strong, and I have no doubt will be so now. I have done every thing to strengthen it and mean to go to Columbia to be at the Election of Electors. The 24 numbers of *the Republican* which I have written have been sent on to you, and I trust you have received and approved them. They are written in much moderation and have been circulated as much as possible. So has the *little Republican Farmer* I shewed you in Philadelphia and which has been reprinted in all our *Southern States*. With these and my Speeches on Juries, Judges, Ross' Bill, the Intercourse Bill and the Liberty of the Press, we have Literally sprinkled Georgia and North Carolina *from the Mountains to the Ocean*. Georgia will be *Unanimous*, North Carolina 8 or 9, Tennessee Unanimous, and I am hopefull we shall also. I suppose you must have got the Volume of my Speeches. One was sent you by Post and another by Water Via Philadelphia. I have done every thing that was possible here and have been obliged *alone* to take the whole abuse of the Parties United against us. They single me out, as the object. My situation is difficult and delicate, but I push Straight on in those principles which I have always pursued, and in which I would persevere if there were but *ten Men* left who continued to think with me.

October 16: 1800

Since the within written we have had the election for Charleston, which by dint of the Bank and federal Interest, is reported by the Managers to be against us 11 to 4—that is the federalists are reported to have 11 out of 15 the number for the City representation. . . . All our intelligence from the Country convinces me, we shall have a *decided majority* in our Legislature. Besides we mean to dispute the Election of Charleston on the ground that many have Voted who had no right and are not Citizens—I am told 200—and that a Scrutiny is to be demanded. . . . I never before this knew the full extent of the federal Interest connected with the British and the aid of the Banks and the federal Treasury, and all their officers. They have endeavored to Shake *Republicanism in South Carolina* to its foundations, but we have resisted it firmly and I trust successfully. Our Country Interest out of the reach of Banks and Custom Houses and federal officers is I think as pure as ever. I rejoice our Legislature meets 130 or 40 Miles from the Sea. As much as I have been accustomed to Politics and to Study mankind this Election in Charleston has opened to me a new view of things. Never certainly was such an Election in America. We mean to contest it for 8 or 9 of the 15. It is said several Hundred more Voted than paid taxes. *The Lame, Crippled, diseased and blind were either led, lifted or brought in Carriages to the Poll.* The sacred right of Ballot was struck at, for at a late hour, when too late to counteract it, in order to know how men, who were supposed to be under the influence of Banks and federal officers and English Merchants, Voted, and that they might be Watched to know whether they Voted as they were directed, the Novel and Unwarrantable measure was used of Voting with tickets printed *on Green and blue and red and yellow paper* and Men stationed to watch the Votes. The Contest lasted several days and Nights and will be brought before the House. . . .

October 26: 1800

Our accounts respecting our State Legislature are every day more favorable. From those We have heard of We are sure now to have a decided majority and We still have to hear from other counties which have been always republican and which in fact we considered our strong ground. I send this under cover to Mr. Madison and am hopeful you will get it safe and unbroken, my Letters have many of them come to me open which obliges me to use this precaution. . . .

November 22: 1800

I have just received your favour after an interval since its date of nearly one Month. I am to particularly regret Your not receiving my communications as I wanted some facts from you to aid me in the very delicate and arduous struggle I have in this state. Finding from my intelligence that the Pennsylvania Senate intended to contend for a concurrent vote in the choice of Electors and thus to shield themselves under a pretended affection for the rights of their branch from the popular odium I very early perceived that the choice of a President would in a great measure depend upon this States Vote. I therefore very assiduously have attended to this Object since June and now wait the Issue which is to be decided on on Tuesday next. My anxiety on this subject is very much increased by a Letter I have received from Governour Monroe in answer to one I wrote him on the subject. He seems to think with me that our state must decide it and that Pennsylvania is very uncertain. . . . I am hopeful we shall succeed and although my situation is truly delicate in being obliged to oppose my own Kinsman, (who does not now on that account speak to me) yet Urged by those principles it is my duty never to forsake and well convinced that the Election depends on this State I have taken post with some valuable friends at Columbia where our legislature meet and are now in Session and here I mean to remain until the thing is settled. I am told I am to be personally insulted for being here while I ought to be in Washington and that a Motion will be made expressing the opinion of one of the Branches that all their Members ought to be present at the discussion of the French Treaty. But I who know that the Presidents Election is of more consequence than any Treaty and who feel my presence here to be critically important, mean to remain and my friends with You who know the reason will readily excuse my absence. To weaken the federal Party in our Legislature which is stronger than I ever knew it an attempt is made to set aside the Charleston Election and I have suggested a new idea to the Petitioners which is to suspend the sitting members immediately from their seats. I inclose You a Petition on the subject which at their requests *I have drawn and they are* now debating it. Whether they vote or not I think we shall carry the Election and the Moment it is decided I will write You. My situation here is peculiarly delicate and singular. I am the *only member* of Congress of either side present and the federalists view me with a very jealous Eye. . . .

December 2: 1800

The Election is just finished and We Have, Thanks to Heaven's Goodness, carried it. We have Had a hard and arduous struggle and I found that as there Were no hopes from Philadelphia and it depended upon our State entirely to secure Your Election and that it would be almost death to our hopes for me to quit Columbia I have remained until it is over and now permit me to congratulate You my dear sir on an Event, which You will find we had an arduous and doubtful struggle to carry and of which I will send You the particulars before I set out. Expect me soon in Washington, but I shall be late, important public arrangements for the republican interest detaining me here a little longer. . . .

28 FEDERALIST LEADERS DISCUSS FUTURE PARTY MANAGEMENT

Taking an introspective look at the Federalist party in the aftermath of its defeat in 1800, Fisher Ames concluded that the situation was not hopeless, and Ames and other Federalists were soon giving con-

siderable thought to party strategy. The plan which Hamilton proposed to Delaware's Federalist Congressman James A. Bayard was not
adopted, but his reflections on the reasons for the Federalist defeat and
his suggestions for the future management of the party deserve notice.
John Rutledge Papers, University of North Carolina; Lodge, ed., *Works
of Alexander Hamilton*, X, 433-37.

Fisher Ames to John Rutledge
January 26, 1801

I hope it is not too late to wrench the name *republican* from those who
have unworthily usurped it. By doing so, we should augment our strength,
which is ever the effect of a successful display of it. Names and appearances are in party warfare arms and ammunition. It is particularly necessary
to contest this name with them now as ardently as the Greeks fought for
the body of Patroclus. The novus ordo Seclorum must not begin with an
impression on the popular mind that we are a disgraced if we are a disappointed party. We must court popular favor, we must study public opinion, and accommodate measures to what it is and still more to what it ought
to be, for that last will remain and uphold us. Spleen caprice and vindictive
feelings are below our party now and the great duties that devolve upon its
leaders. *To oppose* has been an easy task—nobody was answerable for
measures, and few cared about the petite guerre of debates and newspaper
invectives. Lately we had a man at our head who deserted the cause and
assailed his friends and the friends of the country. The state of the Federal
party has been for the last six or eight months unspeakably embarrassing
and without precedent. If the Jacobins should step into power and act
according to their own evil dispositions, they would take our burdens and
disadvantages on themselves. We should enjoy their late advantages or at
least so much of them as our better principles would permit us to avail
ourselves of. By exposing the innovations and hostile designs of the Jacobins we should hold fast with the property virtue and sense of the nation—
and I trust make it appear that though we had lost the helm we had not lost
power over those who hold it. We should appear as strong as ever and
stronger than when our strength was paralised as of late. . . .

Alexander Hamilton to James A. Bayard
April 1802

    . . . I am glad to find that it is in contemplation to adopt a plan of con-
duct. It is very necessary; and, to be useful, it must be efficient and com-

prehensive in the means which it embraces, at the same time that it must meditate none which are not really constitutional and patriotic. I will comply with your invitation by submitting some ideas which, from time to time, have passed through my mind. Nothing is more fallacious than to expect to produce any valuable or permanent results in political projects by relying merely on the reason of men. Men are rather reasoning than reasonable animals, for the most part governed by the impulse of passion. This is a truth well understood by our adversaries, who have practised upon it with no small benefit to their cause; for at the very moment they are eulogizing the reason of men, and professing to appeal only to that faculty, they are courting the strongest and most active passion of the human heart, *vanity!* It is no less true, that the Federalists seem not to have attended to the fact sufficiently; and that they erred in relying so much on the rectitude and utility of their measures as to have neglected the cultivation of popular favor, by fair and justifiable expedients. The observation has been repeatedly made by me to individuals with whom I particularly conversed, and expedients suggested for gaining good will, which were never adopted. Unluckily, however, for us, in the competition for the passions of the people, our opponents have great advantages over us; for the plain reason that the vicious are far more active than the good passions; and that, to win the former to our side, we must renounce our principles and our objects, and unite in corrupting public opinion till it becomes fit for nothing but mischief. Yet, unless we can contrive to take hold of, and carry along with us some strong feelings of the mind, we shall in vain calculate upon any substantial or durable results. Whatever plan we may adopt, to be successful, must be founded on the truth of this proposition. And perhaps it is not very easy for us to give it full effects; especially not without some deviations from what, on other occasions, we have maintained to be right. But in determining upon the propriety of the deviations, we must consider whether it be possible for us to succeed, without, in some degree, employing the weapons which have been employed against us, and whether the actual state and future prospect of things be not such as to justify the reciprocal use of them. I need not tell you that I do not mean to countenance the imitation of things intrinsically unworthy, but only of such as may be denominated irregular; such as, in a sound and stable order of things, ought not to exist. Neither are you to infer that any revolutionary result is contemplated. In my opinion, the present Constitution is the standard to which we are to cling. Under its banners, *bona fide,* must we combat our political foes, rejecting all changes but through the channel itself provides for amendments. By these general views of the subject have my reflections been guided. I now offer you the outline of the plan which they have suggested. Let an association be formed to be denominated "The Christian Constitutional Society." Its objects to be:

1st. The support of the Christian religion.

2d. The support of the Constitution of the United States.

Its organization

1st. A council, consisting of a president and twelve members, of whom four and the president to be a quorum.

2d. A sub-directing council in each State, consisting of a vice-president and twelve members, of whom four, with the vice-president, to be a quorum.

3d. As many societies in each State as local circumstances may permit to be formed by the sub-directing council.

The meeting at Washington to nominate the president and vice-president, together with four members of each of the councils, who are to complete their own *numbers* respectively.

Its means

1st. The diffusion of information. For this purpose not only the newspapers, but pamphlets, must be largely employed, and to do this a fund must be created; five dollars annually, for eight years, to be contributed by each member who can really afford it (taking care not to burthen the less able brethren), may afford a competent fund for a competent term. It is essential to be able to disseminate *gratis* useful publications. Wherever it can be done, and there is a press, clubs should be formed, to meet once a week, read the newspapers, and prepare essays, paragraphs, etc.

2d. The use of all lawful means in *concert* to promote the election of *fit* men; a lively correspondence must be kept up between the different societies.

3d. The promoting of institutions of a charitable and useful nature in the management of Federalists. The populous cities ought particularly to be attended to; perhaps it would be well to institute in such places—1st, societies for the relief of emigrants; 2d, academies, each with one professor, for instructing the different classes of mechanics in the principles of mechanics and the elements of chemistry. The cities have been employed by the Jacobins to give an impulse to the country; and it is believed to be an alarming fact that, while the question of presidential election was pending in the House of Representatives, parties were organizing in several of the cities in the event of there being no election, to cut off the leading Federalists and seize the government.

The foregoing to be the principal engine. . . . In Congress our friends to *propose* little, to agree cordially to all good measures, and to resist and expose all bad. This is a general sketch of what has occurred to me. It is at the service of my friends for so much as it may be worth.

29 PRESIDENT JEFFERSON SEEKS A FLOOR LEADER IN CONGRESS

When John Randolph, chairman of the House Ways and Means Committee, broke with Jefferson in March, 1806, the Republicans were left without a floor leader. Revealing his recognition of the need for effective party management in Congress, the President, July 5, 1806, urged Representative Barnabas Bidwell of Massachusetts to assume party leadership in the House and act as the administration's spokesman. Jefferson Papers, Library of Congress.

I read with extreme regret the expression of an inclination on your part to retire from Congress. I will not say that this time, more than all others calls for the service of every man. But I will say there never was a time when the services of those who possess talents, integrity, firmness and sound judgment, were more wanted in Congress. Some one of that description is particularly wanted to take the lead in the House of Representatives to consider the business of the nation as his own business, to take it up as if he were singly charged with it and carry it through. I do not mean that any gentleman relinquishing his own judgment, should implicitly support all the measures of the administration; but that, where he does not disapprove of them he should not suffer them to go off in sleep, but bring them to the attention of the house and give them a fair chance. Where he disapproves, he will of course leave them to be brought forward by those who concur in the sentiment. Shall I explain my idea by an example? The classification of the militia was communicated to General Varnum and yourself merely as a proposition, which, if you approved, it was trusted you would support. I knew indeed that General Varnum was opposed to any thing which might break up the present organisation of the militia: but when so modified as to avoid this, I thought he might perhaps be reconciled to it. As soon as I found it did not coincide with your sentiments, I could not wish you to support it, but using the same freedom of opinion, I procured it to be brought forward elsewhere. It failed there also, and for a time perhaps may not prevail; but a militia can never be used for distant service on any other plan; and Buonaparte will conquer the world if they do not learn his secret of composing armies of young men only, whose enthusiasm and health enable them to surmount all obstacles. When a gentleman, through zeal for the public service, undertakes to do the public business, we know that we shall hear the cant of backstairs counsellors. But we never heard this while the declaimer was himself a backstairs man as he calls it, but in the confidence and views of the administration as may more properly and respectfully be said. But if the members are to know nothing but what is important enough to be put into a public message, and indifferent enough to be made known to all the world, if the Executive is to keep all other information to himself, and the house to plunge on in the dark, it becomes a government of chance and not of design. The imputation was one of those artifices used to despoil an adversary of his most effectual arms: and men of mind will place themselves above a gabble of this order. The last session of Congress was indeed an uneasy one for a time: but as soon as the members penetrated into the views of those who were taking a new course, they rallied in as solid a phalanx as I have ever seen act together. Indeed I have never seen a house of better dispositions. They want only a man of business and in whom they can confide, to conduct things in the house; and they are as much disposed to support him as can be wished. It is only speaking a truth to say that all eyes look to you. It was not perhaps expected from a new member, at his first session, and before the forms and style of doing business were familiar, but it would be a subject of deep regret were you to refuse yourself to the conspicious part in the business of the house which all assign to you, perhaps I am not entitled to speak with so much frankness; but it proceeds from no motive which has not a right to your forgiveness. Opportunities of candid explanation are so seldom afforded me, that I must not lose them when they occur.

30 PRESIDENT JEFFERSON ON REPUBLICAN FACTIONALISM

Early a problem in American politics, factionalism had critically disrupted the Federalist party while in power, climaxing in a break between Hamilton and Adams. The Republicans, once in office, did not remain so united as they had been in opposition. Republican splits in Pennsylvania and New York were especially serious, and the defection of John Randolph threatened a national schism. Jefferson moved speedily to prevent Randolph's revolt from crippling the party nationally, but he did not involve himself or commit the prestige of his office and party leadership in state or local party divisions. The President's concern over Republican factionalism can be seen in the following letters. Ford, ed., *Writings of Thomas Jefferson*, VIII, 348-49, IX, 129-30; Jefferson Papers, Library of Congress.

To Wilson Cary Nicholas
March 26, 1805

The divisions among the republicans which you speak of are distressing, but they are not unexpected to me. From the moment I foresaw the entire prostration of federalism, I knew that at that epoch more distressing divisions would take its place. The opinions of men are as various as their faces, and they will always find some rallying principle or point at which those nearest to it will unite, reducing themselves to two stations, under a common name for each. These stations or camps will be formed of very heterogeneous materials, combining from very different motives, and with very different views. I did believe my station in March 1801 as painful as could be undertaken, having to meet in front all the terrible passions of federalism in the first moment of it's defeat and mortification, and to grapple with it until compleatly subdued. But I consider that as less painful than to be placed between conflicting friends. There my way was clear and my mind made up. I never for a moment had to balance between two opinions. In the new divisions which are to arise the case will be very different. Even those who seem to coalesce will be like the image of clay and brass. However under difficulties of this kind I have ever found one, and only one rule, *to do what is right,* and generally we shall disentangle ourselves without almost perceiving how it happens.

To Caesar A. Rodney
October 23, 1805

How deeply to be regretted, my dear Sir, is the bitter schism which has lately split the friends of republicanism into two adverse sections in Pennsylvania! It holds up a melancholy prospect to the friends of liberty when they see two descriptions of sincere votaries to republican government let their passions get so far the mastery of their reason and patriotism, as that the one should drive, and the other hand into power the monarchical enemies of both, rather than use a little indulgence towards the opinions of each other. Is all reconciliation impossible? Have personal hatreds obtained such dominion over the breasts of both as to render every other sacrifice preferable? Every patriot on both sides who feels this should retire and suffer their more temperate brethren to come forward and endeavor a reconciliation. . . . He who would do to his country the most good he can, must go quietly with the prejudices of the majority till he can lead them into reason.

. . . I cannot put pen to paper to a member of either party without scolding.

To James Gamble
  October 21, 1807

. . . I have long seen, and with very great regret, the schisms which have taken place among the republicans, and principally those of Pennsylvania and New York. As far as I have been able to judge they have not been produced by any difference of political principle, at least any important difference, but by a difference of opinion as to persons. I determined from the first moment to take no part in them, and that the government should know nothing of such differences. Accordingly it has never been attended to in any appointment or refusal of appointment. . . .

IV PARTIES AND THE PRESS

That both Federalists and Republicans recognized the usefulness of a party press was demonstrated by their efforts to establish party newspapers and by the aid that political leaders gave to party editors. Individuals, party committees, and other groups established and supported party presses, and numerous newspapers made their appearance as the party contest quickened. Although many papers were short-lived, at least 234 newspapers were in publication at some time during the year 1800, and at least 327, in 1808. Despite the attempts of some editors to remain impartial in the party contest, by the time of the election of 1800 the great majority of newspapers displayed a clear party attachment, and a number of them exhibited extreme partisanship. Some editors, such as William Duane of the Philadelphia *Aurora,* Thomas Ritchie of the Richmond *Enquirer,* and James Cheetham of the New York *American Citizen,* became actively engaged in state party politics. When Jefferson took office in 1801, the Federalist press appeared more powerful than that of the Republicans. Thus, throughout his presidency Republican leaders concentrated considerable attention on the establishment and support of Republican newspapers, gradually turning the balance in their favor. By the end of Jefferson's administration, Federalist leaders were desperately trying to instill new life into the Federalist press.

31 JAMES MADISON SEEKS TO AID
EDITOR PHILIP FRENEAU

While Freneau's Philadelphia *National Gazette* (1791-93) was less
important in the growth of the Republican party than many later newspapers, it was prominently involved in early partisan conflict. Jefferson
explained his reasons for aiding Freneau in a letter to Washington,
September 9, 1792 (Document 14 above). Madison, who had conducted the negotiations which led to Freneau's establishment of a paper
in Philadelphia, joined Jefferson in soliciting subscribers, as indicated
in this letter to Mann Page, August, 1791. Dreer Collection, Historical
Society of Pennsylvania.

This will be handed you by Mr. Childs who solicits subscriptions
to a new Gazette to be edited at the Seat of Federal Government from his
press by Mr. Freneau. He will communicate to you the plan, which speaks
its own merits. Those of Mr. Childs having besides other vouchers, the
character and success of a paper of which he has long been the printer in
New York. With Mr. Freneau I have been long and intimately acquainted.
He is a man of acknowledged genius, of extensive literature, of experience
in the business he is to conduct, and of great integrity. These qualifications
promise a vehicle of intelligence and entertainment to the public which has
the best pretensions to its patronage. I take the liberty of asking yours, not
only from a persuasion that in bestowing it you will aid a very useful undertaking, but from a desire of testifying my esteem and friendship for the
conductor of it by contributing to render the profits as proportionate as
may be to the justice of his title to them.

32 ALEXANDER HAMILTON SEEKS TO AID
EDITOR JOHN FENNO

Fenno, editor of the Philadelphia *Gazette of the United States,* was an
early champion of Hamiltonian measures and a veteran of skirmishes
with Freneau's *National Gazette.* The following letters reveal the close
relationship between the editor and the Secretary of the Treasury. Since
Fenno continued to publish his paper, it appears that Hamilton was
successful in answering Fenno's appeal for help. Charles R. King, ed.,
The Life and Correspondence of Rufus King (New York, 1894-1900),
I, 501-2.

Fenno to Hamilton
November 9, 1793

After struggling for four years and an half with a complication of difficulties in supporting my publication, difficulties which no industrious person has perhaps been called to encounter since the organization of the general Government, I am reduced to a situation so embarrassing as incapacitates me from printing another paper without the aid of a considerable loan. The Types which I informed you I had wrote for are arrived. They amount to upwards of 500 Dollars. Debts, which I cannot any longer procrastinate the payment of amount to 1000. It will require 500 to procure the necessary stock of paper etc. to recommence business. A loan of Two Thousand Dollars therefore would relieve me, and not only so, but place me in a situation which would supercede probably the necessity of any further application of a similar kind. By the above statement you will perceive that matters are not altered for the better since the time I submitted a schedule of my Debts and Credits to you, which was last Spring. Tho' I have incessantly importuned my distant subscribers and agents to make payment since the 18th September, I have received only 35¼ dollars; tho' accounts to the amount of 1500 Dollars have been forwarded during the period that has elapsed since. I therefore conclude that tho' I have more than 4000 Dollars due, there is no dependence to be placed on a fund so wretchedly precarious.

I have reserved myself to renew my business. Several eligible berths have been attainable in the Bank of the United States—these are now filled. There are yet some vacancies in the Bank of Pennsylvania—Mr. Fox is about leaving the office of Cashier, and the place of First Accountant is to be filled. I wish, Sir, for your counsel and advice. If the plan you suggested some time since of a subscription can be carried into effect, or if a Loan can [be] made, all may be well. If not, my career as a Printer is closed. Four years and an half of my life is gone for nothing; and worse (for I have a Debt of 2500 Dollars on my Shoulders), if at this crisis, the hand of benevolence and *patriotism* is not extended.

Of the use of the word patriotism, no man can judge with so much propriety as yourself—for no man is so well acquainted with the springs and motives of my conduct. Wishing, Sir, that your health may be firmly reestablished, and apologizing for this intrusion, which nothing but the urgency of the case can justify at this time

I am, sir, most respectfully your ever devoted and humble servant

John Fenno

Hamilton to Rufus King
  November 11, 1793

Inclosed is a letter which I have just received from poor Fenno. It speaks for itself.

If you can without delay raise 1000 Dollars in New York, I will endeavour to raise another Thousand at Philadelphia. If this cannot be done, we must lose his services and he will be the Victim of his honest public spirit.

33 THOMAS JEFFERSON URGES THE USE
OF THE PRESS IN PARTY CONFLICT

Although Jefferson himself did not write for the Republican press during the party contest of the 1790's, he encouraged others to do so and to join him in giving financial assistance to Republican editors. Here, as he did on other occasions, he appealed to Madison, February 5, 1799, to aid the party cause through the press. Ford, ed., *Writings of Thomas Jefferson*, VII, 344-45.

A piece published in Bache's paper [*Aurora*] on *foreign influence,* has had the greatest currency and effect. To an extraordinary first impression, they have been obliged to make a second, and of an extraordinary number. It is such things as these the public want. They say so from all quarters, and that they wish to hear *reason* instead of *disgusting blackguardism.* The public sentiment being now on the creen, and many heavy circumstances about to fall into the republican scale, we are sensible that this summer is the season for systematic energies and sacrifices. The engine is the press. Every man must lay his purse and his pen under contribution. As to the former, it is possible I may be obliged to assume something for you. As to the latter, let me pray and beseech you to set apart a certain portion of every post day to write what may be proper for the public. Send it to me while here, and when I go away I will let you know to whom you may send, so that your name shall be sacredly secret. You can render such incalculable services in this way, as to lessen the effect of our loss of your presence here. . . .

34 A REPUBLICAN EDITOR ANNOUNCES
HIS PARTY ALLEGIANCE

While at the beginning of the 1790's it had been common for editors to profess impartiality even if not observing it, by the end of the decade editors such as Alexander Martin of the Baltimore *American* were publicly proclaiming their party attachments. *American and Daily Advertiser,* May 16, 1799.

To the Public

After encountering an unpleasant train of disappointments which has tended to procrastinate the period first fixed for the appearance of the AMERICAN, the Editor feels no small degree of satisfaction, that he is enabled, even at this *late date,* to lay its first number before the public.—He has already stated in the PROSPECTUS, the politics which shall be supported by his paper:—He feels himself superior to adopting the hacknied, hypocritical protestations of those editors, who *at first,* avow a rigid *impartiality,* and as soon as their papers have gained a circulation, prostitute them to the service of any party which will dispense the *"loaves* and *fishes"* with the greatest liberality—he respects too much the discernment of that public to which he looks for support, to insult it, as *other* Editors have frequently done, by declarations of *neutrality,* while every column of their papers are repleted with party effervescence;—He therefore candidly declares, that the "AMERICAN" shall give an energetic, and undivided support to the *Federal Constitution;* to the principles which led to the *American Revolution,* and to that genuine *amor patriae* which by calling into action abilities the most eminent, the most arduous struggles, and unremitting perseverance, has thus preserved us from a ruinous and destructive WAR; that would be productive of no other effect, than furthering the views of a *corrupt* and *debased Monarchy* in the destruction of *Republicanism,* and the consequent erasure of our own name from off the list of free and independent nations. . . .

The American people have long enough been imposed upon by the pretended impartiality of printers; it is all delusion; every party will have its *printer,* as well as every sect its *preacher;* and it is as incongruous for a publication to be alternately breathing the spirit of REPUBLICANISM and ARISTOCRACY, as for a clergyman to preach to his audience *Christianity* in the morning, and *Paganism* in the evening. . . . Every Editor who is capable of soaring above the flattery of villainy, and the adulation of power has too much at stake, in the contest of liberty against slavery, virtue against vice, and truth against sophistry, to admit of more than a *limited impartiality.*

In supporting the principles of *Republicanism,* the Editor is aware that he shall lay himself open to all the hatred, malice, slander and persecution, which form the leading policy of the advocates of *toryism* and *royalty;* but he pledges himself not to allow them a single inch. . . .

Alex. Martin

May 13, 1799

35 A FEDERALIST EDITOR EXPLAINS
HIS POSITION

The Richmond *Virginia Federalist,* April 30, 1800, edited by William
A. Rind.

It was to be regretted, that in the Metropolis of the important and
extensive State of VIRGINIA, no Federal Printer had appeared, whose
Press had been conducted in a manner which editorial consistency would
seem to require on the one hand; and the Friends of Order, and the General
Government, certainly had a right to expect on the other.

The object of the VIRGINIA FEDERALIST is to remedy this evil.—
Professing our admiration of the manly measures pursued by the General
Government; seeing the beneficial effects which have already been experienced, and considering them as an evidence of their wisdom, that speaks
plainly to the understanding of us all, and happily disproves the gloomy
predictions of those who advised a contrary policy;—professing a deep
rooted hostility to foreign influence of every kind, our efforts will be increasing to maintain harmony among the States; and point the public mind to
UNION, as the best means of securing individual happiness, and the only
all-efficient Guardian of National Independence.

The Paper has now been established about Ten Months, and in the
course of this short period, having obtained a very extensive circulation
through this Commonwealth, as well as in many of the other states,—
besides being a repository of the most valuable political essays, and a
correct vehicle of the most interesting intelligence, both foreign and domestic, will afford a publicity to Advertisements, which cannot fail to obtain it
a preference, especially from gentlemen, whose political sentiments coincide
with those of the Editors, and who conceive a Gazette conducted on the
principles here stated, contributory to the cause of Federalism, and to the
perpetuation of the public happiness.

36 EDITOR SAMUEL HARRISON SMITH
DECLARES HIS SUPPORT
OF THE JEFFERSONIAN ADMINISTRATION

The Washington *National Intelligencer* was the principal newspaper
spokesman for the administration during Jefferson's presidency, and
its editor had close personal contacts with the President. While refusing
to become embroiled in petty party controversies, Smith made clear his

loyalty to the Jeffersonian administration. *National Intelligencer,* October 6, 1802.

Address to Subscribers

On the 31st of this month two years will have elapsed since the first appearance of the National Intelligencer.—During this period much has occurred abroad to awaken curiosity, and much at home to excite interest. The intrinsic importance of the events that have occurred has necessarily and properly produced these effects. It had been well for the national character, if other effects, had not accompanied them. Unfortunately for the peace of society, party violence has burst forth with unbridled fury, and threatens to prostrate the brightest talent and purest virtue of the community.

The transfer of power from one set of men, governed by certain political principles, to another set of men guided by different principles, has kindled a resentment that presides to itself no limits; and too many of our presses, administering to its gratification, are filled with the basest and lowest detraction.

Under these circumstances it becomes the Editor of the National Intelligencer openly and distinctly to assign the rules of his conduct; rules which he has found no reason to abandon, and which it is not probable he will ever relinquish.

Believing the freedom of speech and of the press to be one of the great bulwarks of our liberties, it has been and shall be vigorously sustained. That freedom consists in the temperate discussion of all principles and measures on which the general happiness depends. While, on the one hand, it holds no principle too sacred for examination, it forbids all personal slander and vulgar language. The National Intelligencer, therefore, has not, and will not enter into personal warfare with any wretch who by his crimes has abandoned himself to infamy, nor will it, elated with editorial consequence, make the nation the theatre of the petty feuds of hostile prints. Such falsehoods and follies will be left to their own fate. On the contrary detraction will be discountenanced, and the plain language of truth, whenever it shall be thought necessary, shall put down the slanderer.

Believing that our happiness essentially depends upon a republican government, and that such government is alike susceptible of abuse and improvement, whatever increases a love and respect for it, whatever tends to destroy its abuses or promises its amelioration shall be admitted.

Believing that the measures of the late administration tended to draw into disrepute the republican system by incorporating numerous and dangerous abuses, which were calculated with great rapidity to hurry us into the common vortex of ruined nations, those measures have been held up to public opinion as unworthy of imitation; while the measures of an administration, zealously attached to the republican system, and resolutely bent on keeping this country apart from foreign connection, have been enforced as the offspring of a wise and honest policy.

These measures are well known to the readers of the National Intelligencer, with the arguments urged as well in their opposition as support. Since the establishment of the paper, every document of importance has been given, and the debates of the legislature at a length which, it is believed, is unparalleled. Nor will the malice of party ascribe to them a want of rigid impartiality.

From this exposition, it will be seen that the Editor does not claim an exemption from decided political convictions. However the recluse student may shroud himself in apathy, the citizen of a genuine republic, in the midst of the political scene, must have little sensibility and less patriotism not to embrace with zeal one side or the other. If he believe the general happiness to depend upon the republican system, if he believe that system to depend upon the unimpaired enjoyment of peace, upon the moderation of taxes, and if he believe that the men now in power will insure these effects, while those in opposition would mar them, can he be indifferent? No fellow citizens; while we are moderate let us be vigilant; while we limit ourselves to truth, let us embrace that truth with zeal; and while we desire the happiness of our opponents, let us take care of our own.

So long as the National Intelligencer is conducted on these principles, it may, without presumption, claim the support of the enlightened patriot. That support it already possesses in an eminent degree. But an extended subscription, while it rewarded the Editor, would enable him to improve the plan of the Paper, and to enlarge the sphere of its usefulness. Under this impression, and with this view the Editor requests the person, who shall receive the accompanying specimen papers, to obtain as many subscribers as shall be in his power, on one condition, which experience has proved to be indispensable, the actual payment by each subscriber of five Dollars in advance.

37 VIRGINIA REPUBLICANS ORGANIZE A NEWSPAPER

William Munford, a Republican member of the Virginia House of Delegates, explains to Joseph Jones, of Petersburg, December 1, 1799, the plan by which a group of Richmond Republican leaders established

The Press which began publication in Richmond, January 31, 1800. Joseph Jones Papers, Duke University.

My confidence in your republican principles induces me to suppose that you will with pleasure assist in any judicious and practicable plan to support and propagate those principles in our Country. I take therefore this method to inform you that a Company of Gentlemen have associated to establish a National Republican Newspaper in the City of Richmond, of which I inclose you a Copy of the Constitution, which was framed at a Meeting on the 28th day of last October. Two hundred shares have already been subscribed for, of which I have taken ten, but by the desire of the Trustees, am to dispose of all but one, for the purpose of promoting the advantages of the Institution, by engaging in the undertaking a greater number of Republicans. The object of the Institution is to publish a paper daily or three times a week (according to the state of our funds) in defence of the cause of freedom, which is at present in so much danger. Supported by the Interest of so many proprietors, by the Judgment of such men as the Trustees, and the genius of the Editor, (whom I know to be a man of great talents,) I have no doubt that the paper will be the most valuable and most widely diffused vehicle of information on the Continent, and may greatly tend to give a new turn to the sentiments of the people thro' out the United States. Permit me therefore to request you to take one or more of my shares. . . . I should wish you to take several shares if convenient, and to dispose of them among your friends in Dinwiddie, that the Republican spirit of the people of that County may be kept alive and strengthened by the information which this paper will contain.

38 NEW YORK REPUBLICANS SOLICIT SUPPORT FOR REPUBLICAN NEWSPAPERS

The Republican leaders of Ontario County, New York, included this appeal for support of Republican printers in a *Circular,* Canandaigua, March 23, 1808. While exaggerating the number of Federalist papers, it pointed up the widespread difficulties of printers in collecting subscription payments. Broadside, New-York Historical Society.

We invite your attention to another subject—*the support of the Press.* . . . By the invaluable art of printing, the PRESS has become the vehicle of knowledge—and knowledge the sheet anchor of FREEDOM. Republicans must support their *Presses,* or their Presses cannot support *Republicanism.* If public patronage fail them, designing and wealthy men

will buy them up to mislead and pervert public opinion—then, soon bid
farewell to Freedom! Despots and *would-be* tyrants most fear, feel, and
best know the effects of the PRESS on human society. The federalists and
British partizans have years since correctly appreciated the influence of the
Press on public opinion, and have better patronized it. Their printers acknowledge they are better paid by their party than the Republican printers
are—and we have other evidence—that with the large majority of Republicans in this country, yet there are two Federal papers to one Republican in
it. This is a severe reflection on the Republicans for their remissness; and
we hope it will invite them to extend their patronage by liberal subscriptions
and payments for papers. Let every Republican make it a matter of principle and honor to pay his printer when due, and it would greatly aid him
in his resources. . . .

39 A FEDERALIST CIRCULAR PROMOTES
A PARTY NEWSPAPER IN THE NATIONAL CAPITAL

The Federalists had no paper of national influence which could equal
that of the Republican Washington *National Intelligencer* or Philadelphia *Aurora.* In this circular Archibald Lee and Robert Beverley,
a committee to assist the *Washington Federalist,* explain plans for ex-
panding the services and influence of that paper and seek support from
Federalists throughout the country. Printed circular, Georgetown, September 15, 1808, John Rutledge Papers, University of North Carolina.

The Friends of the WASHINGTON FEDERALIST, having determined
at this momentous Crisis, to make it as useful as possible to the cause it
was erected to support, have lately transferred the Establishment to its
present Editor Mr. FINDLAY, and have directed us, who are nominated a
committee, to confer with the Gentlemen who are similarly occupied in the
restoration of the principles of our great Founder.

The local position of the WASHINGTON FEDERALIST will give it obvious
advantages as a steady Centinel on the measures of the present Administration, and if its efforts are not curbed by the extraordinary expences the
EDITOR must incur to give his press the utmost effect it is susceptible of, we
are well assured it will be rendered the earliest as well as amongst the most
correct Organs of public Information. Its Patrons here have acted with
unusual Liberality towards it, yet are they impressed with the belief that its
ultimate success must depend in a considerable degree upon the aid its distant Friends may furnish it.

Mr. FINDLAY has engaged a Gentleman of Talents to assist him in the

Editorial Duties, and it is proposed to employ a faithful Stenographer to attend sedulously to the reporting of the Debates of the Congress during its Session, a Proof Sheet of which will be furnished each Evening of the same day, to such Editors throughout the Union, as may be disposed to contribute to the extra Expences this Arrangement will give rise to. During the Recess of Congress any important Information that can be gathered at the Seat of Government, Mr. FINDLAY proposes to furnish his Friends in an extra Sheet.

It will be evident that the heavy Expences incurred by the Federal Prints, who now find it requisite to have their Agents to attend the National Legislature, to procure them correct Reports of the Debates, will be superceded by this Arrangement, and that those who have not heretofore enjoyed this advantage, will have it in their power to give to the Public a regular Statement of the Proceedings of Congress, as well as all other Intelligence that the Seat of Government may afford—several days earlier than they can at present.

We request the Gentlemen who act on the several Committees of Federal Affairs to recommend to their States and Friends, this Establishment, and the propriety of supporting it as extensively as possible.

V EARLY PARTY MACHINERY

Formal party machinery was established earliest in the middle Atlantic states, especially in Pennsylvania and New York, where early party divisions were unusually close and the demands of conducting state-wide election campaigns necessitated particular attention to organization. The party contest in the presidential election of 1800 produced the formation of party machinery on a scale never before equaled, contributing significantly to the Republican triumph. Following Jefferson's election, Republicans concentrated extensively on establishing party machinery in the New England states in an effort to break Federalist control in that region. Although the Republicans commonly took the initiative in introducing party machinery, the Federalists generally followed with similar organization, despite their attempts to create the impression that they did not need to resort to the vote-getting measures of the Republicans. The spread of party machinery and increased organizing efforts indicate that parties found such devices useful and successful in advancing their interests—in nominating candidates, conducting election campaigns, gaining new adherents, improving party unity, and, most important of all, winning elections. The party machinery illustrated in this chapter was found on the state, county, and local levels. National party organization consisted principally of the members of each party in Congress and the informal contacts and association of party leaders. Although an impressive amount of formal party machinery was in operation before Jefferson left the presidency, informal organization continued to prevail in some areas, particularly in much of the South and the West.

40 A NEW YORK COMMITTEE OF CORRESPONDENCE ORGANIZES SUPPORT FOR JOHN JAY FOR GOVERNOR IN 1792

The techniques of marshaling voter support and creating party machinery were adapted to state electoral procedures and local political customs. The earliest steps toward party organization commonly involved some system of committees of correspondence such as that indicated in these communications from a committee of party leaders in Albany to influential citizens throughout the state. The first is a letter addressed to David and Peter Van Schaack; the second is a printed circular letter. Van Schaack Papers, Library of Congress; Broadside Collection, New York Public Library.

Albany, March 19th, 1792

Gentlemen

At a late meeting of a respectable number of our Friends in this City John Jay Esquire was nominated as a Candidate for Governor and Stephen Van Rensselaer Esquire as a Candidate for Lt. Governor at the Ensuing Election, and we were appointed a Committee of Correspondence to make known and Support this Nomination. To attain these desirable objects we Earnestly request your hearty Co-operation. Permit us therefore to intreat you to Call a meeting of Such of our Friends in your Town as you Shall Judge proper as Early as possible and endeavor to Unite their Exertions with ours in this Business. We also beg leave to Suggest the propriety of your appointing a Committee with whom we may Correspond relative to the above mentioned objects and thro' whom our Communications may be made known with Greater Certainty and Ease to the whole Circle of our Friends in your Town.

Albany, 13th April, 1792

Sir,

As the day of Election is near at hand, and our opponents are using every exertion to influence the public mind in favor of their candidates, we trust it will not be amiss to address you on that subject. . . .

As to the characters and abilities of the new candidates, we presume nothing need be said. The distinguished services of Mr. Jay, in various offices of the highest importance, and the general good name of Mr. Rensselaer, supercede the necessity of any commendation.—Permit us,

therefore, earnestly to solicit your most vigorous exertions in their favor.—
Our prospects of success are, at present, extremely favorable in every part
of the state—but the final result will depend much on our assiduity at the
Polls.

We must also take the liberty to request your particular attention to the
Poll of your town—to bring forward the electors, and to see that the election is held, and the returns made in strict conformity to the law.

41 A PHILADELPHIA POLITICIAN DESCRIBES
THE TUMULT OVER NOMINATING PROCEDURES

Because a Pennsylvania election law of 1792 provided for the selection
of federal representatives and presidential electors on a general ticket,
some means of nominating candidates on a state-wide basis had to be
devised, and in the process certain rudimentary machinery emerged.
In the following letter, August 19, 1792, an active leader of the Republican interest in Philadelphia, Dr. James Hutchinson, describes to Albert
Gallatin the struggle between those who proposed to decide nominations in a general state conference of "conferees" and those who sought
the arranging of nominations through a committee of correspondence.
The "conferees" were generally considered to represent the Federalist
interest; the "correspondents," to speak for the Republican interest.
Albert Gallatin Papers, New-York Historical Society.

You must have heard before this time, of the various measures
which have been taken by those Gentlemen who have so long influenced the
City Politics to procure a meeting of Conferrees, from the different Counties
in this state, for the purpose of fixing (or as they modestly term it proposing) a ticket for Representatives in Congress, and for Electors of a
President and Vice President of the United States; in this business they have
met with a total defeat; I shall not however detain you by detailing particulars, as Mr. Addison, Mr. Brackenridge and several other Gentlemen from
the westward were in the City, and present at most of the meetings, who
no doubt have given you every necessary information. I shall only therefore
say, that the people are now effectually roused, are determined to support
their independence, and think and act for themselves: Six town meetings
have been held in this City, a plan was concerted by some Gentlemen who
met at a Tavern to appoint conferrees, to represent the City, and to form
a Committee of Correspondence to write to the different Counties in the
state, to solicit their concurrence in the measure, in consequence of this
a general meeting of the Citizens was advertised to meet at the State House,

to sanction this business, at the time appointed not more than 70 or 80 persons attended, a number which those Gentlemen who originated the business deemed insufficient to countenance their proceedings, nothing was therefore done; a second meeting was called, when perhaps about 500 persons attended, and they opened the business by proposing conferrees, Mr. Dallas give some opposition, which occasioned some delay, however a Ward Committee was appointed, who retired a few minutes and reported five names for Conferrees and five names for a Committee of Correspondence, the evening was now so far advanced that it was moved not to go into the choice of persons at that late hour, an adjournment was proposed untill the next evening, which being supported by Mr. Wilson was carried; a General meeting was called the succeeding evening. Hitherto there had been no direct opposition, Mr. Dallas and some others had opposed generally, but did not venture to attempt a rejection of the plan altogether, the conduct however of the leaders at this meeting, gave a very serious alarm, the whole ward Committee was read by Mr. John Wilcox from a paper he had in his hand, it was evident that measures had been predetermined, and that the Citizens were merely called together to sanction them; this attempt to take from them the right of suffrage roused a number, who have [been] inactive for years, it was compared with the Circular letter of some of the same persons on the election of Governor, and a number of us determined to meet and oppose the whole business; the next meeting was very large, they could not be accommodated in the state house, and numbers retired from not being able to find room; the business was opened by Mr. Dallas; moving to expurge every part of the business that related to the appointment of Conferrees, he was opposed by Mr. Lewis and Mr. Wilson who both supported Conferrees, but on different principles, When after a long and full discussion of the business the Chairman (who was Mr. Powell) put the Question, and Conferrees were rejected by at least two to one notwithstanding which he declared that in his opinion a Majority was in favour of Conferrees, this was done twice, when a division was called for which the Chairman refused to grant, a scene of Confusion ensued, he abdicated the Chair precipitately, amid the Hisses of hundreds, and called out that the meeting was adjourned. In this situation the confusion was so great, nothing could be done, except to agree on another meeting, to correct the misstatement of the Chairman, and to finish the business. Accordingly on Monday July 30th a General meeting was called in the State House Yard, upwards of 2000 attended, the meeting was the largest since the year 1779, Mr. McKean we chose chairman, I opened the business, by stating the various attempts that had been made to dupe the people, and moved for correcting the proceedings of the evening before and the mistakes or misrepresentation of the Chairman, and also to expurge all that had hitherto been done, this was carried almost unanimously, the friends to conferrees seeing the disposition of the people made no opposition of consequence at this meeting. The next day Tuesday the 31st, the friends to conferrees called another general meeting at 3 O'Clock in the Afternoon, an hour extremely inconvenient to the tradesmen and Mechanics, they had been however exhorted to attend to prevent those people having any opportunity of sanctioning their measures by the majority of a general meeting, and accordingly on Tuesday afternoon both parties met in the State house yard, the meeting was not equally large with the one of the preceding evening, but was very numerous, in the early part of the meeting the majority was doubtful, and both parties seemed disposed to try their strength in the choice of a Chairman; Mr. Powell and Mr. McKean were first proposed, and various divisions were taken without any decision, when both these Gentlemen declined it; then Mr. Morris and Mr. Barclay were proposed with the same success, various divisions took place without being able to ascertain the majority; in the meantime however our friends were encreasing from every quarter, and tho' the majority in the beginning was doubtful, it soon was manifestly against the Conferrees, in this situation of things the friends of Conferrees retired to the west part of the Yard, and attempted to place Mr. Morris in the Chair, this on being observed by the others occasioned a scene of Confusion, they rushed forward, seized the Chair and table and tore them to pieces, and it was with difficulty *violences of a more serious nature* were prevented, the friends to conferrees soon left the yard, the opponents having finished their business the evening before, the day closed without any farther attempts—the Gentlemen friends to Conferrees had several private meetings, and have sent a Circular Letter by a Committee they have appointed through the several Counties, you may probably have received one, if not you must have seen it in the papers— I forgot to observe to you that on the evening of Monday the 30th after expurging the proceedings of the former meeting a Committee of Correspondence was appointed and we have sent Circular Letters through various parts of the state; Those for Fayette, Westmoreland and Bedford are carried by Mr. Huston, those for Washington and Alleghenny, are carried by Mr. Redick; they will attempt no more general meetings in Philadelphia to appoint conferrees; and I hope our friends in the Country will take care that it is not done in the different Counties; for I have no doubt that will be the next attempt, and possibly in some of the Eastern or Middle Counties they may succeed.

42 HUGH HENRY BRACKENRIDGE PROTESTS
THE INNOVATION OF PARTY MACHINERY

The controversy described above by Dr. Hutchinson ended in a failure to secure general support for any public system of nominations in Pennsylvania, and nominations passed into the hands of the emerging party groupings. The innovation of party machinery to control nominations, either by committees of correspondence or by conferences, provoked, as did nearly every new party development, numerous protests. One of the most articulate dissents came from Hugh Henry Brackenridge, a western Pennsylvania writer. Philadelphia *National Gazette,* August 1, 1792.

It is the happiness of a free government, that every one may speak his mind; which if he did not do, he might forget some times, that he had the privilege. Finding a public question agitated at this time, I shall say what I think, if for no other reason, at least to show that I do think, and have an opinion on the subject: it is that of the appointment of Conferees and Correspondents, for the forming a Ticket for members of Congress, etc.

To such appointment I am opposed; because at no city, town, district, or village meeting, on a partial or short notice, which must be the case, by persons assuming an authority to call a meeting, where no system has been previously laid down, or can be hastily adopted, to secure a fair appointment, a few tumultuously attending, forward and noisy men haranguing, the chairman proposing, or some one bringing forward a ticket, which the bulk do not chuse, on principle of delicacy, to oppose; I say at no such meeting, and all town or district meetings will be such, can an appointment take place which will justly represent the people. Or even if the whole of the citizens should assemble, a thing not to be expected, and ballots fairly taken, so that those appointed were really the choice of the town or district, is it certain that the choice of those at the conference, would be the choice which the people would otherwise have made; because the persons that go forward will have attachments and resentments, interests and partialities, hopes and fears, which those at home know nothing of, but which will be fully exercised when they come to form a ticket, and it will be easy for them when they come back, to frame an apology for the choice made if not agreeable, by saying *they were the only names that would go down with the conferees of other districts.* The fact is, that envy or jealousy of equal or superior abilities will unavoidably operate at any such conference to preclude men of merit. Such a conference may be justly styled a junto

or cabal; and I never found truth, honour, justice, or generosity with such
yet. It is the circumstance that makes men act and be what they are, and
it is a good request "lead us not into temptation, but deliver us from evil."
I judge from my own feelings, and know that were I at a conference at this
moment there are those whom I would oppose, just because I do not like
them; they have injured or insulted me, and I hate them, though the people
that sent me know nothing of it, and have no suspicion but that I would
make the same choice that they themselves would make. If all men would
speak the truth, they would say that the case with them would be the same.
The people therefore at the town or district meeting, put themselves in the
power of the passions of the conferees and do injustice to those persons
whom they would otherwise have chosen.

A ticket once put up is not easily taken down; and therefore the act of
the conferees will unavoidably have an influence, tho' it deserved to have
none; because though the citizens might never have thought of proposing
yet they may be unwilling to oppose the names brought forward; and the
bare annunciation is an advantage which the names in the ticket have in
their favor; so that it may be hopeless to oppose, and to bring forward
others in the face of this advantage.

The appointment of conferees, therefore, becomes, on these principles,
an invasion of the right of the citizens at large to think, judge and act for
themselves in the first instance. It is a fraud by one neighbour on another,
the choice being brought forward by a machinery of chusing, in which one
may acquiesce and another not. Leave it to every man to frame his ticket,
or be immediately instructed by others how to do it; but let it be his own
act, and there is no deception, or injustice.

But more especially the appointment of conferees becomes *an invasion
of the rights of those who are or may be candidates,* being a forestalling of
the public choice; a pre-occupying the minds of the people, and not leaving
it on the broad basis of a general and unbiassed vote.

I shall be asked then, by what means, on the present principle of state
election, shall the electors in the different districts fix upon names for
the purpose of a ticket. They may chuse for themselves with respect to a
member or two from their own quarter; but how for members for other
quarters of the state? The method is natural, simple, and easy. There are
gazettes in this city; there is a gazette in almost every town or village
through the state. Let any man who offers his service to the public, announce his name in these as is done every day in Virginia, Maryland, and
other places; or let some one who knows his abilities and inclination,
announce it for him; and of those announced let the people take their
choice.

As to correspondents, I have the same objection to such committees as to those of conferees. It is not always that they judge well with whom to correspond; especially when the distance is considerable. I have seen papers in the western country addressed to persons, and myself among the rest, some of which associates I disdained, knowing them to have just about as much interest in our politics as a brindled cow, and no more. I could not conceive how in the name of God they had ever heard of them; and I mention this to shew how little even the most intelligent men at a distance know whom to consult, and on whom to depend for influence or information; the fact is, they are in the power of persons who may have a temporary life and come forward in affairs, and have relations or supporters, that have consequence with them, but with no one else.

In the business of elections it is my wish, that the light of knowledge with respect to men and characters may shine naturally and equally, and though like the sun, it may be clouded or obscured in places by shade of trees or accident of wind and weather: yet the chance is much more in favour of real merit than from any adventitious help of lenses by which mathematicians might attempt to increase the sun's rays, or direct them where they are not. Were it, in nature, to be left to them, we should not have an equal sun, and taking their passions into view, some would have all day, and others all night. I would scarcely trust David Rittenhouse himself with such a glass, though the best man in the United States; but I would rather leave it to the sun, who, as far as I can recollect, has for several thousand years past, given heat to all alike, and the plant in the wilderness has an opportunity of growing as well as that in the gardens of the botanists.

I feel myself interested on this question; not that I have any object at present of being a member of Congress, or elector of presidents; but the day may come when I may; and I would not wish myself precluded by any system that may be now adopted, and become the custom, which I do not think will be favourable to me or any one who thinks more of the public opinion than of that of particular persons.

43   A PLAN FOR REPUBLICAN PARTY ORGANIZATION IN PENNSYLVANIA

The presidential election of 1796 and the gubernatorial election of 1799 were accompanied by extensive Republican organizational efforts in Pennsylvania. These instructions were adopted by a caucus of Republican legislators, both state and national, and other party leaders meeting in Philadelphia in March, 1799. Printed circular enclosed in

a letter from Tench Coxe to Albert Gallatin, April 12, 1799, Gallatin
Papers, New-York Historical Society.

*The Committee of Arrangement made Report, which was read, and
after amendment adopted in the following words:*

I. That a Corresponding Committee to consist of Generals Muhlenburg
and Irwin, Messrs. Miles, Leib, Penrose, Coxe, and Dallas, be appointed.

II. That the Corresponding Committee select some prominent character
or characters, in each county, for the direction of their Correspondence,
that such characters be intrusted with the diffusion of information through
his county, if it should be deemed expedient.

III. That meetings of citizens be encouraged in each county, for the
purpose of animating each other to exertion, extending their sphere of influence, communicating with each other on the object of the election, and
concentrating the republican interest.

IV. That the members of the Federal and State Legislatures, and such
other confidential characters as may be met with, furnish to the Committee
of Correspondence the names of such persons, in their respective districts
or counties, with whom correspondence should be held.

V. That the citizens should be urged to be particularly attentive to the
election of honest and independent men for Inspectors and Judges, and
that firm and intelligent individuals should be chosen to attend at each
place of election in the respective districts, to ensure fair play, in receiving,
boxing, and returning the ballots, the individuals so chosen to make report
to the Committee of Correspondence of any irregularities which shall occur.

VI. That every citizen should be requested to attend with tickets on the
ground of election, and to exert himself 'till the election shall be closed;
and that previous regulations be made in each election district for preparing
and distributing the Republican Ticket.

44   THE ORGANIZATION OF REPUBLICAN
MACHINERY IN VIRGINIA

In order to prevent the possibility of a single Federalist electoral vote
in the state in 1800, the Jeffersonian-controlled legislature replaced
the district system of electing presidential electors with a general ticket.
The demands of conducting a state-wide campaign led to the creation
of the party machinery described to Jefferson by Philip Norborne
Nicholas, chairman of the central committee. The machinery was put
into motion by a communication from Nicholas to the chairman of
each county committee, February 1, 1800. Jefferson Papers, Library
of Congress; Richmond *Virginia Argus*, March 25, 1800.

Nicholas to Jefferson
February 2, 1800

Colonel Monroe informed me that he had inclosed you a copy of the republican ticket. This of course communicated to you the change which has taken place in the law of this state upon the subject of choosing electors. The members of the legislature before they dispersed adopted a general system of correspondence through the state for the purpose of giving effectual support to our ticket. A committee of five is established in each county and a central committee of the same number in Richmond. The objects of their establishment are to communicate useful information to the people relative to the election; and to repel every effort which may be made to injure either the ticket in general or to remove any prejudice which may be attempted to be raised against any person on that ticket. I was appointed by the meeting who organized the system which I have described as chairman of the general committee in Richmond. We have begun our correspondence with the subcommittees, and mean to keep up a regular intercourse upon the subjects which may seem to require it. Among the duties enjoined upon the general committee, that of writing to the different persons who compose the republican ticket, and informing them that, they are selected on account of their attachment to republican principles, is a primary and most important one. We have received an answer as yet from no gentleman but Mr. [George] Wythe, who consents to occupy a place upon our ticket. This I rejoice at as it will give it great weight and dignity. And I cannot but augur well of a cause which calls out from their retirement such venerable patriots as Wythe and [Edmund] Pendleton. . . .

Instructions to County Committees
February 1, 1800

Inclosed you will receive a copy of the proceedings of ninety-three members of the legislature and a number of other respectable citizens, convened for the adoption of the means, best calculated to give support to the republican ticket. . . . This object is to be effected, by repelling every effort which may be made by persons adverse to the republican interest, either to misrepresent the principles of the law upon this subject, or to excite prejudices against the persons who compose the republican ticket.

If anything should occur in the several counties, which in the opinion of their committees may be prejudicial to the general interest, they will communicate it to the general committee in Richmond, who will take such measures as appear to them adapted to remove the evil.

The committees in the counties will, in communicating with the general committee, address their letters to Philip Norborne Nicholas, *without annexing the word Chairman;* this is enjoined to avoid interruption in their correspondence.

The committee have only to observe further, that you are considered as chairman of the committee of your county; and it is recommended that you forthwith call a meeting of your committee, and notify to the general committee in Richmond, as early as possible, their willingness to co-operate in promoting the republican ticket.

45   VIRGINIA FEDERALISTS ALSO ORGANIZE

Although Federalists denounced Republican organizational methods and tried to create an image of being superior to such tactics, Republican machinery was frequently imitated by the Federalists. This is indicated in a circular from the Federalist central committee in Virginia to county committees. Broadside, Virginia Historical Society.

RICHMOND, SEPTEMBER 22, 1800

SIR,

WHETHER we shall succeed, or even (which is very important) appear a respectable minority, in the ensuing election, will depend almost entirely upon the active zeal of the county committees. They are relied upon for furnishing the written tickets, which may be required in their several counties; the distance, and shortness of time, precluding all assistance from us in this matter. By their exertions too, it is expected that all, who are disposed to vote favorably, will be induced to attend the election.

To effect these essential purposes, it may be necessary to convene the most influential federalists in your county, and in conjunction with them to divide the same into several precincts; to each of which should be alloted such characters as can be confided in, to prepare, and distribute, our ticket amongst their neighbours; and to bring forward all the federalists within their precinct, to vote on the day of Election.

I AM YOUR MOST OBEDIENT SERVANT.

WILLIAM AUSTIN, Secretary.
By order of the committee entrusted with the Ticket of the Minority.

46 THE REPUBLICAN ASSOCIATION OF HUNTERDON COUNTY, NEW JERSEY

In a number of counties in New Jersey, Republican (also named Democratic) associations were organized in the early 1800's. The plan for the Republican Association of Hunterdon County illustrates this type of organization. The preamble is suggestive of some of the practices that occurred in New Jersey elections. Trenton *True American,* January 17, 1803.

Whereas, in some parts of the county illegal and unjust practices were made use of in the late election by the officers appointed to conduct the same, such as collecting votes in the streets, receiving votes by proxy, and taking the votes of Aliens, of persons under age, of non-residents, of married women, of paupers supported by the town, of blacks not possessing the property required by law, and of actual slaves; and as our respectful petitions to the legislature for an investigation of the subject of complaint, and a redress of our grievances, have not been attended with the desired effect. . . .

And as in our Elective Governments it is of the first importance that the voice of the people should be fully, freely, and fairly expressed in the choice of their rulers . . . *Resolved,* That we will use every practicable exertion to prevent the recurrence of such abuses of our elective rights as were practiced at the late election; that we will endeavor to prevent the admission of such persons to vote as are not duly qualified by the Constitution and Laws of the State; and that we will endeavor to obtain at the next election a full and fair expression of the public voice, according to the rules and regulations prescribed by the Constitution and the Laws of the State. . . .

And in order the more effectually to attain the objects stated in the foregoing Resolutions we do hereby associate ourselves together under the title of *"An Association for the preservation of our Elective Rights, and for the support of the Government of the State and of the United States,"* and do agree to the following Rules and Regulations for our government:

I. The Associators of the respective townships shall assemble in their respective townships twice in every year, viz. on the second Saturday of February, and the second Saturday of August, and, after choosing a chairman to preside and preserve order, and a clerk to record their proceedings, shall elect a standing committee of as many members as may be thought proper, and shall transact such other business as may appear necessary for the promotion of the objects of the association.

II. The Standing Committees thus chosen in the several townships shall hold their appointments until the next stated meeting, and shall be eligible to a re-election. In case of the death or the resignation of any Member, the standing Committee of that township shall elect one to supply his place.

III. The Standing Committees of the several townships shall attend, at the general meeting of the Associators of the County, once a year, viz. on the Saturday preceding the day of nomination, to confer and agree upon a ticket for County Representatives and Officers, to be composed of men friendly to our General and State Governments, and to the purity of Elections; and shall publish such ticket, when agreed upon, by a majority of voters present, for general information, signed by the Chairman and Clerk of the meeting.

IV. The standing Committees shall have power to call a general Meeting of the Associators of their respective townships, by advertising or otherwise, whenever any emergency may in their opinions require it; and shall use every lawful and honest means in their power to promote the objects for which this Association is formed.

V. The chairmen of the several Township Committees shall constitute a committee of correspondence, which shall meet four times a year, viz. on the last Saturdays of April, July, October, and January, and confer together upon Measures necessary to be taken to promote the objects of this institution.—It shall also be the duty of the members of this Committee to correspond with similar Associations, and with individuals in this and other counties of the state, and to communicate to each other, and to their respective township committees, all interesting information that they may receive or can collect.

47   THE HIGHLY ORGANIZED PARTY MACHINERY IN BUCKS COUNTY, PENNSYLVANIA

The Bucks County Republican machinery represents the most advanced, rather than the most typical, county party organization in Pennsylvania. The following communication indicates both the maturity of party development found in some areas and the problems of successful party operation. Philadelphia *Aurora*, February 23, 1803.

The Republican Committee of Bucks County, to Their Constituents

Friends and fellow citizens,

We congratulate you on the progress and happy effects of republicanism, in the county, in the state, and in the union. . . . At the late election, the few federalists, that remain in this county, did not attempt to set up a county ticket; perceiving their cause to be hopeless.

. . . How was the happy change effected? With pride and pleasure we reply, that *the appointment of committees to diffuse information, and unite the votes of honest men had a principal effect*. And suffer us to add, that it is by a perseverance in the same system, that you will continue your power and influence, and so the happiness of your country.—Time was in this county, when a few men met at a court, erected themselves into a committee, and assumed the power of forming a ticket for the county. A few others constituted in like manner, formed, perhaps, a counter ticket, and left to the citizens at large, only a choice of two evils. More rational—more consistent with the true spirit of liberty, the plan adopted by republicans. Our tickets are formed agreeably to the representative system; by men elected and specially appointed to the service. A few years ago, when the tickets thus formed, "fell still born to the earth," the election of the committee was rightly judged, to be a matter of small importance, and was ill attended. But now that our tickets are invariably sanctioned by the votes of the people, the committee may be said to hold in trust the whole elective powers of the county; and consequently the election of the committee itself, becomes a matter of high concern and should be fully attended. Has this been the case? It has not: and hence some symptoms of disunion among republicans at the two last elections. You have seen republicans marshalled against republicans—federalists going between; fomenting the quarrel. . . .

We have hinted the reason why some republicans have dissented from your tickets, in one or two instances. *These tickets were formed by committees, chosen in such a manner, as to render it doubtful, whether they spoke the sense of the majority.* The members in some townships were chosen by a very few votes; and these perhaps given by a candidate and his friends. In the following resolutions you will find a complete remedy for the evil, provided you will co-operate in carrying them into effect. The plan of election proposed, will diminish expence and trouble, at the same time that it combines the votes of a majority of the republicans, in chusing future committees. Still you will please to remember, that no committee, however perfectly constituted, can form a ticket to please you all. . . . When therefore a ticket is recommended, which you do not wholly approve, ask yourselves the question, "shall I support this ticket which contains one or two names which I do not like; or shall I break the bond of republican union: sink myself and party into political insignificance and contempt: and see tickets prevail from year to year, containing not a name that I can approve?" An occasional sacrifice of private opinion to public duty, you must make, or your opinion on politics will presently stand for nothing. . . .

Resolved, That the republican committee of Bucks county shall hereafter be chosen, at the same places, and on the same day, as township officers are chosen, viz. the third Saturday of March in every year, between the hours of 4 and 8 o'clock P.M.

Resolved, That the election shall be published and conducted in manner following, viz.

1. The secretary of the committee for the time being, shall give notice thereof ten days before, in one or more of the public papers, which circulate generally in the county.

2. The members of the committee for the townships respectively shall give the like timely notice thereof, by written or printed advertisements, set up in four or more public places in each township.

3. At the time and place, two judges of the election, and one secretary shall be chosen, and they or any two of them shall decide on the qualifications of the electors, shall cause the election to be fairly conducted, and certify under their hand the name of each person chosen.

4. Each township shall elect one, two, or three members, at their discretion: but in fixing the ticket for the general election, each township shall have only one vote: And if the members for any township are equally divided and cannot agree, such township shall lose its vote.

5. The election shall be by ballot, but before it proceeds, each elector present, shall have an opportunity of putting on nomination, as many candidates as he thinks proper.

6. At this election, every person shall have a right to elect and to be elected, who is entitled to vote at the general election, provided he professes to be a democratic republican, and has supported the character for at least six months then last past.

7. If upon counting the ballots it shall appear, that two or more candidates have equal votes, the electors shall immediately determine the preference by a new ballot, or otherwise.

8. From and after the said third Saturday in March, the powers of the preceding county committee shall cease and determine, and the committee chosen as aforesaid, shall hold its first stated meeting at the public house now kept by Josiah Addis, on the first Tuesday of September then following, at 10 o'clock in the forenoon. At this meeting a nomination shall be made of candidates to fill the several elective offices, of state representatives, sheriffs, coroners, and county commissioners; and also of state senator and representative for congress, when occasion requires; and each member shall have a right to put on nomination who, and as many as he pleases; provided that any person nominated, shall have a right to withdraw his name.

9. The committee shall cause publication to be made, in one or more of the current news-papers, of the nomination aforesaid; and of the time and place of fixing the ticket; and they shall accordingly meet at the same

place, or at Dunlap's tavern, on the third Tuesday of the same month; and shall, between the hours of three and six o'clock P.M. chuse by ballot, out of the candidates nominated as aforesaid, the number to be voted for at the succeeding general election.

10. When members of congress are to be chosen, conferrees in behalf of this county shall be elected by the committee on the said third Tuesday of September, seasonable public notice thereof being previously given, and we advise, that the conferrees from this and the other counties concerned, meet at Hartzel's tavern, in Northampton county, on the fourth Tuesday of September; and fix the ticket for representatives to congress. When the committee conceive that this county is entitled to furnish a candidate for congress, they may by ballot, or otherwise, fix the candidate; and instruct their conferrees to endeavour to have his name placed on the ticket.

Resolved, That extra meetings of the committee may be held when six members from three townships shall think it expedient; but in this case the meeting shall be convened at or near the centre of the county; and ample notice thereof shall be given by the public prints, circular letters, or otherwise. *Other* adjourned meetings may also be held; but at such extra or adjourned meetings, no measures shall be taken, which may affect the formation of the ticket for the general election.

Signed by order of the committee,

JOSEPH HART, Chairman
SAMUEL D. INGHAM, Secretary

Newtown, Feb. 8, 1803

48 REPUBLICAN MACHINERY IN MASSACHUSETTS

The following report of a congressional district nominating convention shows an early well-developed system in New England, where Republicans were especially active in the early 1800's. Note the use of the party press and the publication of a brief platform. The activities of Republican county committees were summed up by Dr. Nathaniel Ames, a member of the Norfolk County Republican committee. Printed circular, American Antiquarian Society; Charles Warren, *Jacobin and Junto, or Early American Politics as Viewed in the Diary of Dr. Nathaniel Ames, 1758-1822* (Harvard University Press, 1931), 226.

SALEM, *September* 24, 1802

SIR,

AGREEABLY to a previous notice a Convention of Delegates was held at Danvers, on 22d instant to nominate a Republican Candidate for Essex

South District, as a member to the eighth Congress. At this meeting the
Candidate was voted for by ballot, and on counting the votes it was found
that

THE HON. JACOB CROWNINSHIELD,

was UNANIMOUSLY chosen as the Republican Candidate. The Convention
afterwards resolved themselves into a Committee for the purpose of expressing their wishes to their fellow citizens. . . .

The Convention have therefore unanimously adopted the following resolutions, which they earnestly recommend to your attention.

1st. Resolved, That previous to the election the list of voters be inspected
by the Republicans of every town, and care be taken that no legal voter
be excluded from the list, and no illegal one admitted on the list.

2d. Resolved, That every exertion be made to support the Republican
candidate, by appointing committees, by distributing newspapers, by refut-
ing objections, and by supplying with votes the various wards of every town.

3d. And for the purposes of giving information to the people, as well
as counteracting the arts of imposture—Resolved, That the Printer of the
SALEM REGISTER be requested to print an extra number of papers from
this time to the time of election, to be distributed GRATIS among the people
by the committees of the various towns, and that these committees be
EARNESTLY REQUESTED to send by all opportunities to Salem for the same,
in as great a number as they can use advantageously, and that the same be
delivered to said committees FREE OF EXPENCE.

4th. Resolved, That it be most seriously recommended to all Republicans
to exert themselves to obtain subscriptions for THE SALEM REGISTER,
as a free and well conducted paper, devoted to the republican cause—and
particularly that the committees interest themselves in this behalf.

Such are our importunate and unanimous requests. We have already
engaged the printer to carry into effect the third resolution—and we entreat
you to make the freest use of the privilege—We shall value your attention
in this respect as highly important to the cause, and honorable to yourselves.

Finally, we hold as the creed of Republicans—Freedom of speech—freedom of the press—the right of trial by jury—the union of our states—
the right to elect all officers—inviolability to the constitution—just confidence in government—equal privileges, and equal laws—no expenditures
but by appropriations of law—no summary tribunals—no nobility—no
powers independent of the people—In one word, we hold that liberty is
the birthright of mankind, and a Democracy its only sure preservative.

We believe we shall have the hearty co-operation of the citizens of
——————————— in diffusing these principles—and we trust their triumph

will be secured by the election of a Republican Member to represent us in Congress.

  . . . *Signed in behalf of the Delegates* . . .

Joseph Story, Secretary   John Hathorne, Chairman

Diary of Dr. Nathaniel Ames

Aug. 28, 1808. At a convention of Republicans from all the towns in the county of Norfolk, Cohassett excepted, James Mann, Nathaniel Ames, Nathaniel Ruggles, Samuel Bailey, Abner Crane, John Ellis and John Swift, Esquires, were appointed a County Committee to communicate with the Central Committee of the State, viz. Hon. Aaron Hill, Perez Morton, Samuel Brown, Charles P. Sumner, William Jarvis, Esquires, and Town or subcommittees to watch over the Republican interest both in State and National Governments, especially as to elections and appointments—convey intelligence—confute false rumors—confirm the wavering in right principles—prevent delusion of weak brethren—and fight that most formidable enemy of civilized men, political ignorance, a task, mighty, endless and insuperable without funds to excite, support and disseminate the fruits of patriotic genius—and with the most ample funds will prove a Herculean labor enough to stagger common undertakers to combat the pulpit, the bar and host of superstition, vanity, pride, and selfish wretches under foreign influence, that never had a conception of searching out principles or seeking the truth, and will neither read, see nor hear anything contrary to their own narrow prejudices, wholly actuated by the impulse of the moment.

49 THE REPUBLICAN STATE MANAGER OF CONNECTICUT ISSUES INSTRUCTIONS

The thorough preparations for elections and the highly centralized Republican party structure by 1805 in Connecticut (where Federalism was more powerful than in any other state) is indicated in this circular, a copy of which fell into Federalist hands and was published in the Hartford *Connecticut Courant,* November 27, 1805.

Middletown, Nov. 1, 1805

SIR,

  AS you are appointed, by the general meeting of Republicans, sole manager for the county of Middlesex, and have pledged yourself for the faithful performance of your trust, I take early occasion to address you on the subject of elections, and on the services which are expected from you.

A majority can relax its exertions occasionally without hazard: a minority must exert its full strength constantly. A majority can afford to lose a thousand votes; but a minority ought never to lose a single vote, to which it is fairly entitled.

We have many obstacles to encounter: every republican ought to do his best towards overcoming them. Those, who talk against federalism through the year, and yet neglect to attend proxies, do worse than nothing. Those, who profess to be republicans, and yet vote for federalists on any occasion, do us irreparable mischief. Federalism cannot be talked down or flattered down; IT MUST BE VOTED DOWN.

If we succeed to gain over a small majority, that will soon become a large majority. There is a great number of men in the state, who will always float with the tide. If we can gain a governor or lieutenant governor, or even one in the nomination for congress, all the rest will soon follow. This has been the case in New-Hampshire and in other states, where our cause has prevailed.

By the last returns of nomination for council it appears that we give 8 votes to every 11 votes of the federalists. With such exertions as we might have made, several of the highest on our ticket would have stood on the nomination next spring. WE CAN AND OUGHT TO DO BETTER.

In the discharge of your trust you will notice in all the towns of your county the causes of deficiency, and exert yourself to remove them. In some very republican towns we ought to gain an addition of at least 100 votes. In towns nearly balanced the absence of one or two republicans has lost for us an election, and even our friends, who were disappointed, have left the meeting, without voting for higher offices. In towns, where there are few republicans, our friends are remiss, because they cannot carry the representatives.—This is all idle: every vote, given for the higher offices, is important to us; but a little negligence or some paltry excuse costs us too dear. THERE MUST BE AN END OF SUCH INDIFFERENCE.

For this purpose, I ask you, *immediately after the receipt of this,* to appoint in each town of your county, an active, influential, republican manager, who will assure you verbally or in writing, that he will faithfully discharge his trust.

The duties of a TOWN-MANAGER will be,

1st. To appoint a district manager in each district or section of his town, obtaining from each an assurance that he will faithfully do his duty.

2d. To copy from the list of his town the names of all male inhabitants, who are taxed.

3d. To call together his district managers, and with their assistance to ascertain,

1st. The whole number of males, who are taxed.

2d. How many of the whole number are freemen.

3d. How many of the freemen are decided republicans.

4th. How many————decided federalists.

5th. How many————doubtful.

6th. How many republicans who are not freemen, but who may be qualified at the next proxies.

4. The next duty of the town manager will be to furnish each district manager with the names of all those republicans, who are within the limits of his district. The list of male inhabitants and all proceedings in each town are to be kept by the town manager in a book, from which all his returns are to be made, as herein after directed.

It will be the duty of the DISTRICT MANAGER to exert himself to cause young republicans to be qualified for the oath; also to bring forward the republican freemen in his district at freemen's meetings and other town meetings, as occasion may require: also to furnish them with votes. The list of candidates, as agreed on at the general meeting, will be sent seasonably into every town. The representatives, to be set up in each town, and other town officers will be nominated in such way, as the town and district managers shall agree. . . .

At every Freemen's Meeting it shall be the duty of the Town and District-Managers to assist the republican applicants for the oath, also to notice all objections to admit republicans—also to know the state of the votes for all classes of candidates. They shall also notice what republicans are present, and see that each stays and votes, till the whole business is ended. And each District-Manager shall report to the Town-Manager the names of all republicans absent, and the cause of absence, if known to him, which reports shall be entered in the book for a memorial. . . .

At the general meeting of republicans in May next, it will be my duty to report the whole number of male persons in the state, who are taxed—the whole number of freemen—of republicans—of federalists and of doubtful men. I must also report what hindrances have been given to our cause in any part of the state, either by false reports, by political sermons, by official influence, by refusals to admit freemen, by federal tricks at elections, or *by negligence of republicans*. I must also report the conduct of each class of managers.

On each County Manager I must rely for correct information under each of these heads: they must rely on Town-Managers, and these last on District-Managers. With the last the returns must begin and must be punctual.

As I have power to remove County-Managers and supply vacancies, they have power to do the same in respect to Town-Managers, and these last to do the same as to District-Managers. Formerly responsibility was too much divided: now each one knows the part assigned to him, and if he has the least idea of neglecting it, he must refuse his appointment at once.

I have pointed out some general and indispensible outlines on duty. All subordinate things are left to discretion. The town and district managers will begin their work directly, and will be particular to see that all deeds, left for record, to be relied on for qualification, be actually recorded before the 7th of December next, because in four months from that day, viz. on the 7th of April next, proxies will come, whether we are sleeping or waking.

You will be supplied with newspapers for every town, which the town managers will distribute to the district managers, and these will circulate them among the republicans and federalists in their districts. A correct knowledge of our cause and of our objects will go a great way towards removing the prejudices, which the devices of our enemies have produced on the honest, laborious and most useful part of the community.

The federalists have priests and deacons, judges and justices, sheriffs and surveyors, with a host of corporations and privileged orders, to aid their elections. Let it be shewn that plain men, without titles or hopes of offices, can do better than the mercenary troops of federalism.

Your appointment of each Town-Manager will be accompanied with a few printed copies of this for his use and that of the District-Managers. These will serve as a guide for the opening of the business, and you will give additional instructions afterwards as occasion may require. PROMPT SERVICES AND PUNCTUAL RETURNS ARE INDISPENSIBLE.

ALEXANDER WOLCOTT,

State-Manager

50 FEDERALISTS ORGANIZE IN NEW ENGLAND

Although more successful than the Republicans in keeping their confidential party circulars out of the newspapers, Federalists, while lamenting Republican practices, secretly set up organizations of their own. The following communication from the Federalist state committee of Connecticut to county committees [1805] displays many similarities to Republican procedures. Baldwin Family Papers, Yale University.

Impressed with the Importance of Unity of Action among all the Friends to our ancient establishments, in opposing the Designs of those who would introduce a new Order of things, We feel it our Duty, in discharging the trust reposed in us, as the State Committee, to recommend to you for

communication to the Committees of the several Towns in your County,
the following plan of operation, as most likely to insure the attainment of
an Object so desirable, as the Stability of our Government, and to prevent
the confusion and the mischiefs which must result from the contemplated
change.

We rely with confidence on the good sense, virtue, and energy, of the
Friends of Order in this State, provided their exertions, are called forth
and directed by unity of action. We indeed deeply lament, that existing
circumstances should require the adoption of any measures of this kind.
We admire the simple unbiassed Freedom of election, which has heretofore
so greatly honoured the freemen of this State; and happy would it be for
the people, if no innovation had ever been made. But experience has taught
us, that an inferior party may by combination and concert carry their
measures against the will of an inactive, or disunited majority; and that such
evils can be successfully opposed in no way, but by united counsels and
exertions. If then we have aught that is dear to us, or worth preserving in
our Government, or State Institutions, if we wish to prevent the evils we
fear, it is evident we must sacrifice private views and prejudices, to the
general Interest, and resolve to pursue in unison the following measures,
which a General Meeting of the Federal Interest have on deliberation
thought proper to adopt, and through us to recommend.

That the Town Committees, as early as may be, procure an exact list of
all the Freemen in their respective Towns, arranged under two heads—
Federal.—Democratic. This list they should keep on hand; and as new
freemen are admitted, their names should be added, the numbers on each
to be sent to the County Committees, and a return of the numbers in all
the Towns in the county be sent to the State Committee. This will shew the
Strength of parties in each Town; and also the strength of parties throughout the State; and it is confidently believed, that the Federal Interest in most
of the Towns, and in the State in general, will be found more powerful,
than is generally supposed. Let this consideration be an incitement to
activity and perseverance. The Town Committees should associate with
themselves, a number of the most active, sensible, and Judicious men in
their respective Towns, to aid them. When a freemens Meeting approaches,
the Town Committees should arrange the names of all their Federal freemen in their respective Towns, and draw off 6, 8 or 10 names upon separate
slips of paper, requesting some one trusty person to take such a list, and
engage to call on each man named upon it, and request him, laying aside
all excuses, to attend freemens Meeting, to be there at the opening of the
Meeting, and to stay and vote until the business of the day is finished. This
will secure us an encrease of many thousands of votes. The necessity of it

therefore should be earnestly pressed upon the freemen, by all the motives which the nature of the case furnishes.

Nominations, and the names of those in nomination, who are to be voted for at the particular Meeting, either for the Council, or for Congress, should be distributed to the freemen, at the time they are called upon to attend Freemen's Meetings;—In this way they will learn the general arrangement, and will be prepared to vote *alike* thro' the State.

The town Committees should make lists of all the young men in their respective towns, who are or may be, qualified to be admitted Freemen, and see that they are admitted.

Seasonable attention should be paid to the Qualification by Deed, the Law requires a Deed to be recorded *at length, four calendar months* before the Freemens Meeting.

The Town records should be examined from time to time, to see if any fraudulent attempts are making, by pretended conveyances of Land, to qualify new Democratic freemen. The town Committees should pay particular attention to young men that are coming upon the Stage, that they may be early engaged on the side of truth and sound principles; and that they may be guarded against the errors and delusions of Democracy. This is a most important point, and requires great prudence and attention.

If any falsehood, misrepresentation, or embarrassment should exist in any particular Town or place, the operation of which may be unfavourable to the good Order and Government of the State, and favourable to the cause of Democracy, early information of the facts and circumstances of the case should be made by the Town Committee, to the County Committee, and if necessary, by the County Committee, to the State Committee, that a remedy may be provided if possible. And generally that the Town Committees Communicate to the County Committee, and the County Committees to the State Committee, all such facts and information as may be useful to the Federal Cause.

51 FEDERALIST MACHINERY IN MASSACHUSETTS

In the following Federalist circular the names of the county, the town, and the committeemen were added by hand on a printed form, which was also published in the Republican Boston *Independent Chronicle,* March 28, 1805, with a notation that similar letters were circulating throughout the state "issued from some central dictating caucus of monarchists." This completed circular, signed by the Barnstable County committee, is in the Broadside Collection, Massachusetts Historical Society.

The Subscribers have been appointed a Committee for the County of *Barnstable* by a Meeting of Federalists, in Boston, assembled from all parts of the Commonwealth, to communicate to you a system for making the most effectual arrangements to secure the re-election of our present worthy Governor, and to prevent the administration of affairs from falling into the hands of men, whose violence and inexperience, will endanger the prosperity and happiness, which the good people have enjoyed, under their present rulers. We therefore request you to use your endeavours to carry into effect, within your own town, the following project.

1st. You will, as soon as possible, procure a meeting of the following gentlemen . . . who have been nominated, as above mentioned, a Committee for the town of *Yarmouth*.

2d. At such Meeting the said town Committee will be pleased, *First,* to divide said town into districts, and procure a list of all voters in the town unquestionably Federal. *Second.* To procure a list of all doubtful characters. The object of the first list is, that the Federalists may be known and brought to town meeting. The object of the second list is, that the men may be known, who may be influenced by correct information to vote on the federal side.

For the above purposes, the town Committees are to appoint one or more persons, as a sub-Committee, for each district or division. The members of the sub-Committee to be active, prudent, popular federalists.

Each sub-Committee man is to be furnished with a list of all voters *of the first List,* which are within his division, and to use his exertions for their attendance at town meeting, on Election Day.

3d. The members of both the town Committees and sub-Committees are to exert themselves industriously for the disseminating such information as they may possess, and such as may from time to time be sent to them, among the persons on the list of doubtful characters, and, in general, to take all fair means to convince them of the justice of the federal cause. This is highly important, as it is only from the class of honest and mistaken men, that we can hope to increase the number of federalists; and probably with these much may be done, by proper exertions.

4. The town Committees are requested to report to us the names of the sub-Committees. They will also be pleased to inform us, or either of us, of any particular falsehoods and delusions prevalent in their town, to the end that they may be contradicted or exposed.

5. As the success of these exertions, for the public good, in some measure, depend upon secrecy, we therefore recommend to the town Committee, to be silent even with federalists, and with the sub-Committees on the subject

of their connexion with us, the county Committee; in order that the exertions, in every town, may appear to originate in said town. This is thought to be necessary, in order to prevent jealousies and unfounded prejudices.

We regret that we are compelled, by necessity, to resort to any measures to preserve the commonwealth from the dangers and confusion of innovation, besides those, which result from the natural and unsolicited exercise of the right of suffrage. . . . But the intrigues, the arts, the falsehoods, and the perseverance of our opponents leave us no choice. They are drilled and disciplined with the regularity of an army, and their plans can be counteracted only by equal organization. . . .

52 NEW JERSEY FEDERALISTS SEEK
TO MOBILIZE

The revival of Federalism in New Jersey in 1808 is indicated by this printed circular signed by six members of the Federalist committee of correspondence, New Brunswick, October 21, 1808. Broadside Collection, New Jersey Historical Society.

Understanding that it has been determined to make an exertion throughout the State in support of FEDERAL CANDIDATES at the ensuing election, for members of Congress and Electors of President and Vice-President; a numerous and respectable meeting of the Federalists, held in this City, have appointed the subscribers a Committee of correspondence on that subject, and to assure their federal brethren, in the different counties, that nothing shall be wanting on their part to ensure success.

By the change in the publick opinion, by means of township committees, and a subdivision of townships into minor districts, wherein persons have been appointed to ascertain, from the tax list, the names and number of federal voters, and to bring to the poll those within their respective limits, the majority in Middlesex has been encreased from about 40 to 340.

We invite you, sir, and the federal gentlemen in your vicinity, to adopt similar measures, without delay, and to use your utmost influence to arrange and prepare for this important election, in which, from the best calculation, we shall, undoubtedly succeed, if the exertion be general.

It will be useless for one part of the State to be industrious, while others are supine. We, therefore, rely with confidence on your active endeavours in the arduous struggle, and request a communication of the proceedings and prospect of success in your county.

VI THE NATIONAL NOMINATING CAUCUS

In 1796, Republican members of Congress reportedly held a caucus to consider a candidate to be supported for Vice-President with Jefferson, whom Republican consensus had made the presidential candidate, but no agreement was reached. In 1800, however, a Republican nominating caucus met and named Aaron Burr to be supported for Vice-President with Jefferson on the Republican ticket. So influential was this caucus that every Republican elector who voted for Jefferson also voted for Burr in 1800. The system thus inaugurated was used successfully by Republicans to nominate presidential and vice-presidential candidates until 1824, when for the first time the caucus nominees failed to get elected. The Federalist members of Congress also held a nominating caucus in 1800, but the party's membership in Congress was so weakened by the Jeffersonian triumph that the practice did not continue. Although both parties tried to keep their caucuses secret in 1800, subsequent Republican nominating caucuses were publicly reported and their proceedings published in the newspapers. From the beginning, the caucus came under attack, and controversy continued as long as the system was used. Yet, despite challenges, the caucus nominated presidential and vice-presidential candidates for a quarter of a century.

The caucuses of 1804 and 1808, which can be best documented, will serve to demonstrate how the system operated and how it was attacked and defended.

53 A CONGRESSMAN REPORTS THE CAUCUS OF 1804

Jacob Crowninshield, a Republican Representative from Massachusetts, attended the caucus of 1804 and here reports briefly on the proceedings to Barnabas Bidwell, February 26, 1804. Henry W. Taft Collection, Massachusetts Historical Society.

I just steal a moments time to tell you that the republican members of Congress held a caucus last evening when we *unanimously* agreed to recommend Mr. Jefferson as President at the next election. Upon balloting for the Gentleman to fill the office of Vice President (108 members present, being all the republican senators and representatives now in Washington) it was found that Governor [George] Clinton of New York had 67 votes the remainder being scattered amongst Messrs. Breckinridge, Lincoln, and Langdon. Mr. Clinton having thus a very handsome majority he will be recommended to the Electors as the most proper person to fill the Vice Presidential chair. Mr. Burr had not one single vote, and not a word was lisped in his favour at the meeting. He returned to this place two days since and I presume must be much mortified at this decision.

54 A VIRGINIA REPUBLICAN OBJECTS TO THE CAUCUS AND IS ANSWERED BY A PARTICIPANT

Littleton W. Tazewell, an active Virginia Republican who had served in the state Assembly and briefly in Congress, received little sympathy from John Randolph when he protested against the 1804 Republican caucus, in which Randolph had participated. Tazewell Family Papers, Virginia State Library.

Tazewell to Randolph
March 4, 1804

How fast is this government of ours settling into aristocracy; and into an aristocracy of the worst kind, the aristocracy supported by Intrigue. The people although nominally still possessed of the authority and power of the government, in fact have no interest whatever, except in Congressional elections. When these are made, they become a mere tool in the hands of their Representatives, compelled to execute whatever they decide. The manner of your late proceedings conclusively proves these positions. An unauthorized meeting undertake to decide, that one of the old Servants of the people is no longer worthy of their confidence. Without specifying any charge against him, or offering any proofs to support it, they offer to the public choice a new candidate of their own selection. What is the consequence? The people are compelled to elect this candidate so thrust upon them, or run the risk of splitting among themselves, and thereby permitting the election of a man whose political tenets differ altogether from their own. An intriguing character has nothing therefore to perform, but to secure the good will of a majority of the majority of the members of Congress, and his success is inevitable. Nay the Intrigue becomes more dangerous from the manner in which it is conducted. If the proceedings of this Caucus were open, and the sentiments of each of its members necessarily known, there would be a degree of responsibility attached to their actions, which would render them liable to fewer objections. But instead of this, they decide without debate, and nothing is known but the result of their decision even to themselves; burying thus all sort of responsibility in the secrecy and confusion of a ballot box. . . .

Randolph to Tazewell
  April 21, 1804

Your remarks on the mode in which men are brought forward to public notice are forcibly striking. Yet, as you cannot devise a remedy, it appears to be one of those inherent evils of our system (for what system is without them) to which we must submit. Instead of railing at the thing, I wish you would come and participate in it. . . . Cabal is the necessary effect of freedom. When men are left free to act, we must calculate on their being governed by their interests and passions. . . .

55   THE NOTICE CALLING THE CAUCUS OF 1808

Stephen R. Bradley, Senator from Vermont, who had presided over the 1804 Republican nominating caucus, called the 1808 caucus by means of this printed invitation. Edwin Gray Papers, Duke University.

SIR,

IN pursuance of the power vested in me as president of the late convention of the Republican members of both houses of Congress, I deem it expedient; for the purpose of nominating suitable and proper characters for President and Vice President of the United States for the next Presidential election; to call a convention of the said Republican members, to meet at the Senate chamber on Saturday the 23d instant at 6 o'clock P.M. at which time and place your personal attendance is requested, to aid the meeting with your influence, information and talents.

Dated at Washington, this 19th day of January, A.D. 1808.

S. R. BRADLEY

56 REPRESENTATIVE EDWIN GRAY PROTESTS THE SUMMONING OF THE CAUCUS OF 1808

Among those Republican Congressmen who protested against Senator Bradley's action in summoning the caucus, Representative Gray of Virginia was perhaps the most outspoken in this letter addressed to Bradley, January 21, 1808. It should be noted that Gray was a staunch supporter of Monroe for the nomination that was expected to go to Madison in the caucus. Edwin Gray Papers, Duke University.

Your proclamation dated the 19th instant and addressed to me, has been received, and I take the earliest moment to declare my abhorrence of the usurpation of power declared to be vested in you—the mandatory style —and the object contemplated therein.

I deny that you possess the right of calling upon the Republican Members of Congress, or others at this time and place, to attend a Caucus for the Presidential election.

You must permit me to remind you Sir, that it was a far different purpose for which my Constituents reposed their confidence in me. I will not consent either in an individual or representative capacity, to countenance by my presence, the midnight intrigues of any set of men, who may arrogate to themselves the right, which belongs alone to the people, of selecting proper persons to fill the important offices of President and Vice President —nor do I suppose that the honest and unsuspecting people of these United States, can, much longer suffer in silence, so direct and palpable an innovation upon an important and sacred right, belonging exclusive to them.

57 SENATOR JOHN QUINCY ADAMS REPORTS THE CAUCUS OF 1808

A Federalist in the process of becoming a Republican, Adams attended the Republican nominating caucus in 1808 and recorded the event in his diary. Charles Francis Adams, ed., *Memoirs of John Quincy Adams, Comprising Portions of His Diary from 1795 to 1848* (Philadelphia: 1874-77), I, 504-7.

[January 20, 1808] . . . Mr. Bradley delivered me a printed (circular) invitation to attend the meeting of the *republican* members of both Houses, Saturday evening, at six o'clock, to consult respecting the next presidential election. He observed to me that he hoped the old gentleman, Mr. Clinton, would be complimented with a *unanimous* vote for re-election as Vice-President, though he did not expect he would serve. I asked whether he was not to be supported for the Presidency. He said no; he was too old; and we are all witnesses that his faculties were failing; that Madison was the man for the Presidency. I agreed to attend the meeting.

[January 23, 1808] . . . I dined with Mr. Bradley at his lodgings, and in the evening attended the convention of members to nominate suitable persons as candidates for the offices of President and Vice-President. There has been much question as to Mr. Bradley's authority to call this convention, which it seems he contends was given him at a convention on the last presidential election, four years ago. The New York members especially are extremely averse to it. There were, however, about ninety members who assembled under Mr. Bradley's summons; upon which he stated the authority formerly given him, and his reasons for calling the meeting. But he said that, as exception had been taken to his exercise of that authority, it was now at an end, and the meeting must proceed at their own pleasure. He said that he had issued his circulars to every republican member of both Houses; indeed, to every member, excepting *five* of the Senate and twenty-two of the House of Representatives. Nor should I have omitted them, said he, but that they have never been in the habit of acting with us. Mr. Giles moved that Mr. Bradley should take the chair; which he accordingly did. It was agreed that the members present should be counted, and Mr. Milledge and Mr. Varnum were appointed tellers. The number present was found to be eighty-nine. Mr. Bradley proposed the appointment of a clerk. Mr. Burwell and Mr. G. W. Campbell were successively chosen, and excused themselves from serving. Mr. Johnson, of Kentucky, was then chosen, and accepted. After some question whether there should be a viva voce nomination and a subsequent ballot, it was at last agreed to vote by ballot without nomination. On taking the ballots for the office of President, there were eighty-three votes for James Madison, three for James Monroe, and three for George Clinton. Before the ballot for Vice-President, Mr. Pope made a speech recommending unanimity for the choice of this office. The votes were seventy-nine for George Clinton, five for Henry Dearborn, three for John Langdon, and one for J. Q. Adams. The chairman then declared James Madison duly nominated, by a great majority of votes, as a candidate for the office of President, and George Clinton for that of Vice-

President. A committee of correspondence was then chosen, consisting of a member from each State; but Connecticut and Delaware, not being present, had no members chosen. A resolution was then offered by Mr. Giles, and adopted, for publication, stating this nomination, and the reasons which induced the meeting to make it, after which the meeting adjourned without day, and I came home. Many of the persons who attended this meeting thought it precipitately called. Many refused to attend. The number present was a bare majority of the whole number of members. Twenty-seven fed-eralists were not invited; about sixty others were absent, among whom were all the Virginian, or Randolph minority. Dr. Mitchell told me that Bradley's ardor in favor of Madison was stimulated by his personal views, and that he was now soliciting offices for his son, and for his brother-in-law, by the name of Atwater. From the appearances at the meeting I judged it to be called in concert, and probably at the instigation of the Virginian Madi-sonians, and particularly Messrs. Giles and Nicholas. I suppose their par-ticular object to be to aid the canvass of Mr. Madison's friends for electors of President and Vice-President, which is now going on in the Virginia Legislature.

58   THE CAUCUS OF 1808 EXPLAINS ITS ACTIONS

After balloting, the caucus of 1808 adopted the following resolution introduced by Senator William B. Giles. From proceedings published in the Washington *National Intelligencer,* January 25, 1808.

Resolved, As the sense of this meeting that James Madison of the state of Virginia, be recommended to the people of the United States, as a proper person to fill the office of President of the United States, for four years from the 4th of March, 1809; and that George Clinton, the present Vice-President, of the state of New York, be recommended as a proper person to fill the office of Vice-President for the same term. That in making the foregoing recommendations, the members of this meeting have acted only in their individual characters as citizens; that they have been induced to adopt this measure from the necessity of the case; from a deep conviction of the importance of union to the Republicans throughout all parts of the United States, in the present crisis of both our external and internal affairs; and as being the most practicable mode of consulting and respecting the interests and wishes of all, upon a subject, so truly interesting to the whole people of the United States.

59 THOMAS RITCHIE DEFENDS THE CAUCUS

In the public debate over the caucus, editor Ritchie published this editorial under the heading "My Own Opinions" in the Richmond *Enquirer,* February 2, 1808.

. . . Some objections have been made to the recommendations of the caucus at Washington, and some efforts have been made to detract from the weight of that measure. I believe, for my own part, that this system is not absolutely destitute of objections; but the only reasonable question is, where is there a *better* plan? The members of Congress have just as much right (as citizens) to recommend a President and Vice-President, as the republican delegates of Virginia have to frame an electoral ticket. There *must* be some plan to produce a concert and harmony of operations between men of the same party, or else their influence will be *lost by division,* and their enemies will *conquer* by superior prudence.

The Representatives of the people may be presumed to carry with them the wishes of the different quarters of the union.—They express this collective result not in their legislative character but in the unassuming capacity of simple citizens. In what better way can this nomination be accomplished? If it be devolved on every individual of the country, then the inhabitants of each state would be divided about their favorite candidate. If it was referred to the members of the state legislatures, then different states acting independently and without concert would have their different candidates. No candidate would ever obtain a majority of the electoral votes, at least in times like the present, when no one candidate stands proudly conspicuous and unrivalled. The probability then is that the *States* themselves would have in all cases the election of the President. Now, what objections can be made against an original recommendation by the individual members of congress, which may not be urged with ten fold force against the dernier election by Congress in its electoral character? But there is this lamentable difference between the two cases; that in the former Virginia enjoys its full weight of influence and numbers; whereas in the latter, she sinks to the same level with the little state of Delaware. In the former case her influence is as 24 to 176; in the latter as 1 to 17. . . .

60 JAMES MADISON'S OPPONENTS DENOUNCE THE CAUCUS

Led by John Randolph, a staunch supporter of James Monroe, seventeen members of Congress who favored either Monroe or George

Clinton issued a statement opposing the caucus nomination, closing with this strong protest. Washington *National Intelligencer,* March 7, 1808.

We do therefore in the most solemn manner protest against the proceedings of the meeting held in the Senate Chamber on the twenty-third day of January last, because we consider them—

As being in direct hostility to the principle of the constitution:

As a gross assumption of power not delegated by the people, and not justified or extenuated by any actual necessity:

As an attempt to produce an undue bias in the ensuing election of President and Vice-President, and virtually to transfer the appointment of those officers from the people, to a majority of the two Houses of Congress.

And we do in the same manner protest against the nomination of James Madison, as we believe him to be unfit to fill the office of President in the present juncture of our affairs.

61   IN DEFENSE OF THE CAUCUS

While an individual's position in regard to the caucus was frequently determined by his opinion of the candidate nominated, the caucus as a method of party operation was also examined on its own merits. A particularly thoughtful analysis was presented by the New York "Young Republicans" in an *Address of the General Committee of Republican Young Men, of the City and County of New York* (New York: 1808), adopted August 2, 1808. Pamphlet, New-York Historical Society.

The nomination of President and Vice-President of the United States, made at the City of Washington, in January last has excited among us an agitation which no similar occurrence has produced; though it was to have been hoped, that at the present juncture of our national affairs, it would have met with at least the *usual* acquiescence.

To this nomination, various objections are raised. Some to the proceeding itself, and others, (which if solid would be infinitely more serious) to the character and fitness of the candidate for the Presidency.

That objections should at this day be urged against a mode of nomination which has so long met the concurrence and approbation of the people—which has always appeared to them the *best* means of securing a judicious selection, and which experience proves to have been attended with such beneficial consequences to the union and safety of the Republican party, did at first surprize us not a little. . . .

That no party can long exist without concert among its members, and a unity of object and pursuit; and that these are to be obtained only by a ready submission of *private opinion,* to the will of the MAJORITY, are truths universally admitted. How to ascertain this will for all practicable purposes of legislation and government, has ceased to be a question in the United States.

Whilst two parties divide us, differing on *cardinal points* of policy and administration, to effect the election of a President and Vice-President of their choice, must always be to either a matter of the first importance. In the REPUBLICAN PARTY, the necessity of selecting a *single* candidate for each of these offices, to whom the PEOPLE may be directed in their choice, has never yet been disputed. *How* this selection is to be made, whether by *committees appointed specially for the purpose,* or by the *Representatives of the People in Congress,* PROVIDED THE WILL OF THE MAJORITY BE KNOWN AND PURSUED, cannot, we think, be in any wise material. In every instance hitherto, that trust has been reposed in the *Representatives* as the most convenient mode, and least liable to unnecessary expence and delay: and because, in the talents and honesty of those to whom our dearest interests are already confided, we expect to meet the surest pledges of its wise and faithful execution. The sanctioning voice of their constituents has hitherto proved, that this expectation has *never* been disappointed.

If then it be *necessary* for the union and safety of the Republican party, that this trust should be *somewhere* delegated, and if the Representatives of the People, at Washington, are as likely as any other body to execute it, (and have in fact in other instances executed it) with wisdom and fidelity, objections to this nomination must arise from causes *unconnected* with the MODE, and which would apply with equal force to individuals acting under any other form of delegation. That vague and undefined charges of *corrupt motives* and *undue influence* have been made and reiterated, is undoubtedly true; but it is equally true that *bold assertions* are not FACTS nor *angry accusations* PROOFS.

Let us see whether the nature of the case does not prove to the dullest understanding, that such charges are utterly unfounded. Of CORRUPTION *in its grossest sense,* it is unnecessary to speak, for granting (what cannot be granted without a blush) that *eighty-three* members of Congress *could* be purchased, where was the *individual,* where the *treasury* rich enough to purchase them? If by *undue* is meant *official* influence, where, how, and by whom could it have been exercised? Certainly the rod of power was not suspended, nor did an armed force besiege the capitol. Mr. Jefferson was about to retire from his station, and to resign that influence which that station gives him, (and the influence of his character and opinion as a wise and good man, who could wish to abridge?), and by this *very nomination,* if approved and confirmed by the people, that very official influence was to be *transferred.* The nominators did not meet in secret cabal at midnight, and in a desert; no menaces were used to deter, no force to compel a vote.—Openly in the face of day, in the midst of a populous city, a meeting was convened to which *every republican member* of Congress was invited, and at which *eighty-nine* did actually attend, and the decision of that meeting was the result of an almost *unanimous* vote.

It appearing, therefore, from facts undisputed and indisputable, that there was nothing unfair or improper in the *proceedings* of the nominations. . . .

VII CAMPAIGNING FOR OFFICE

The development of political parties had important effects on the methods of seeking office. Although local political customs and traditions continued to influence campaign practices, one noticeable innovation was the growing approval of the idea that campaigning for office by the candidates themselves was acceptable political conduct. In general, electioneering was more direct in the southern and western states than in the middle states and New England, but everywhere the growth of parties brought both necessity and respectability to electioneering. Whether a candidate issued an address to the voters over his own name or left this to be done by a party committee, whether a candidate himself campaigned or relied on an election committee, the voters were increasingly solicited for their suffrages. Independence of party had once been considered a desirable political attribute, but by the end of the 1790s party affiliation had become almost essential to political success. Campaigns for office rang with appeals for support for the party ticket, and party loyalty became a test of political orthodoxy.

To study the activities of candidates seeking political advancement is to be reminded that political parties rested upon the successes of those individuals seeking office and that their election in turn rested upon their ability and that of their party to obtain mass popular support. The means to that end were sometimes subtle, sometimes crude, but the final decision was always left to the American voter.

62 REPRESENTATIVE JOHN PAGE OF VIRGINIA DISCUSSES THE CONDUCT OF A CONGRESSIONAL CANDIDATE

John Page, a member of the first four Congresses, argued against campaigning for election in any fashion. While Page reflected a view common in the early 1790's, few candidates maintained this position at the end of the decade. *An Address to the Citizens of the District of York in Virginia*, June 20, 1794, Virginia State Library.

. . . I have thought it derogatory to the dignity of constituents, in a republic, where the rights of man are understood, and the doctrine of equality asserted, that Representatives should adopt practices used in countries, where those rights and that doctrine are neither understood nor tolerated. Courting popularity as it is called, and attempting to gain the affections or *votes* of the people, is so nearly connected with an officious attention to them, and an unwearied effort to gratify their curiosity or their wishes, that any one of the citizens of these United States who is acquainted with the history of mankind and the frailty of human nature, will agree with me, that the more attention I pay to my business in Congress, and the less to my constituents, the greater must be my respect for them, their dignity and permanent interests. For such a man must know, that courting popularity has oftener produced tyrants, or demagogues, and revolutions attended with confusion and slaughter, than patriots and good government: that the man, who to suit his purpose, has been most zealous in serving the people, has often been most insolent in trampelling on their dearest rights; and that he who viewed his fellow citizens as incapable of being seduced into error, or as too dear to him, to run the risk of proving them capable of such weakness, has always been found most worthy of their confidence. I know I may be asked here, how are our fellow citizens to receive information respecting the proceedings of Congress and the conduct of their Representative, and how are they to be acquainted with his real character, if he be so delicate as not to mix with them, nor address them by speaking or writing, for fear of appearing to aim at popularity? To this I reply, that they have a right to expect from him a general account of the *important* transactions of Congress—and such accounts as the newspapers and journals contain of their proceedings—but, that even this, should be discretionary with a Representative; for he should be allowed to be a judge whether the newspapers which he may have to transmit to them contain a true state of facts; and whether indeed, he can give even the general account above mentioned, without interfering too much with his duty in Congress. . . .

As to harangues in public, I have on a former occasion declared to you "that I am not qualified by habit, or education to harangue you: and that if I were so qualified, I should not be fond of countenancing a practice, which might in time expose electors to the mortifying reflection, that they had preferred an orator to a statesman, flashes of wit to sound judgment, and empty words, to substantial proofs of genuine patriotism." I do not therefore think that public verbal addresses, can be relied on as a criterion by which a representative's character can be ascertained and fixed. Perhaps nothing is more fascinating and delusive than oratory: I will take the liberty of adding that nothing is so apt to impose upon the understanding of men not acquainted with its magic powers, and qualified by education to distinguish between reality and appearances, truth and fiction, sophistry and sound reasoning. And perhaps less dependence ought to be put on written addresses, as the means of discovering the talents and character of a candidate or representative, than on verbal—because the man who can act well the orator's part, amongst his constituents may be supposed qualified to take an active part in debates—but the man who only writes addresses may possibly only copy what he sends amongst constituents, and may be incapable of composing two sentences of his address: indeed this may be the case of some orators, for they may deliver admirably an oration which they may be utterly incapable of composing. But the misfortune is, that the greater the abilities of the candidate or representative may be, both as an orator or a writer, if he should chuse to impose upon his constituents, with more ease and certainty would he impose on them—more readily could he seduce them into a belief of his virtue and patriotism—If neither public harangues, nor written addresses are to be relied on as means of discovering the real character and abilities of a representative; perhaps still less so, is private conversation, or mixing freely, and frequently conversing with his fellow citizens. For here, there is such a field for dissimulation, and the seducing arts of insinuation and address, which some men have eminently possessed who could neither write addresses nor deliver orations if written for them; that it must require more discernment than most men possess, and a longer time than the public welfare will admit of to see through, and find out the real characters of men of dissimulation, cunning and address. But if frequently visiting the electors were required of Representatives, the strong, healthy, active and rich alone could possibly go through the business. . . .

But to return to the question, how are our fellow-citizens to be acquainted with the true character of a Representative? I answer, by enquiring of persons who know him well, and who have understanding and discernment sufficient to see through the artifices of designing men; to distinguish real from apparent worth; and whose integrity and veracity may be relied on: by enquiring of disinterested persons respecting the general tenor of his public conduct, and examining into the debates and journals of Congress.

I have been thus full and free my dear countrymen and fellow citizens, because I think it of the last importance to the Liberty and Independence of our country, that the election of Representatives should be as free as possible from any personal influence of a candidate, arising from his frankness of manners, polite and elegant address, from his eloquence in harangues, or from his skill and facility in writing letters and addresses. His experience in public business, his ability to transact it; his attachment to his native country, to his district, and to the United States; his knowledge of their true interests; his independence and firmness of spirit; his integrity, and delicate regard for his reputation, should be the object of enquiry respecting the character of a candidate: and the man possessing these qualities and dispositions, should be nominated, and voted for, whether he should offer himself as a candidate or not.

63 NEW JERSEY ATTEMPTS TO DISCOURAGE ELECTIONEERING

This excerpt from the New Jersey election law published in the Newark *Centinel of Freedom*, October 5, 1796, is suggestive of political practices and abuses at election time. Laws restricting treating and other electioneering practices were found in various states but nowhere seem to have been rigidly enforced.

. . . *And be it further Enacted,* That if any Candidate shall, at any such Election, or previous thereto, solicit any Elector or Electors, either personally, or by Letter, Message, Advertisement or otherwise, to nominate him or to vote for him; or if any Person whatsoever shall, at any such Election, give offer or promise any Fee or Reward, Victuals, Drink or other Consideration, to or for the Use of any County, City, Township, Precinct, or Body politic or corporate, or by Bribery or Corruption endeavour to prevail on any Person to nominate him, or to vote for him, or to nominate or vote for any other Person or shall appear at such Election with any Weapons of War, or Staves or Bludgeons, or Use any Threats that may tend to put any of the Candidates or Electors in Fear of personal Danger, or shall otherwise endeavour to intimidate, or by indirect Means persuade any Elector to give, or to dissuade any Elector from giving his Vote for the Choice of any Person, or shall make any false Assertion, or Propagate any false Report concerning any Candidate, with a View to prevent his being elected, or that shall have an evident Tendency thereto, or shall summons or request any Party of Militia to attend at the Time and Place of Election, every such Person shall, for every such Offence, forfeit and pay the Sum of Twenty Pounds. . . .

64 A NORTH CAROLINA FEDERALIST OFFERS FOR OFFICE

Although considered improper in many states, self-nomination by candidates was an accepted practice throughout the South. Broadside, July 1, 1800, North Carolina Department of Archives and History.

To the Freemen of Fayetteville District

THE Partiality of a considerable Number of the Citizens of our District, had induced them frequently to request that I would become a Candidate for its Representation in Congress. I have hitherto declined their Invitation, as well from a Persuasion that it would operate a material Derangement of my private Concerns, as from a Belief that the Interests of the District would not be assisted by my superceding the Gentleman who is its present Representative.

But as these Solicitations are again repeated, I am willing to comply with the Wishes of my Friends; and do, therefore, although at this late Hour, come forward as *a Candidate for the Representation of the District of Fayetteville in the House of Representatives of the Congress of the United States*—Solemnly engaging (if elected) to protect and extend your Interests, as far as may be within the Power and Compass of my Talents.

To those of my Fellow-Citizens with whom I have not a personal Acquaintance, and who may not therefore be informed of my Political Principles, it may be necessary to state, that I am what the Phraseology of Politicians has denominated a *FEDERALIST*. But, although I am *the Friend of Order, of Government, and of the present Administration,* I will not pledge myself to support, in Consequence of a selfish, or a bigoted Policy, any Governmental Measure which I might think pernicious to the General Welfare of our Country, or the particular Interests of yourselves.

I am, very respectfully,
Your obedient Servant,
SAMUEL D. PURVIANCE

Fayetteville, July 1, 1800

65 A NEW ENGLANDER DEPLORES THE CONDUCT OF ELECTIONS IN BOSTON

Boston *Mercury and New-England Palladium*, February 10, 1801.

The present mode of electing to the most important stations (which by our excellent constitution is committed to the people) is in the town of *Boston* attended with many evil consequences of serious importance. The assembling so large a number of persons of different habits of thinking, different modes of address, variant and even opposite in their political sentiments and views, each ardent in his own cause, in one place, and at one hour, necessarily produces much confusion wrangling and even uproar. The truth of this will not be questioned by any person, who has attended our electoral town-meetings for the last four years. The crowd upon the stairs leading to Faneuil Hall, is generally on those occasions, so great as to endanger the limbs and even the lives of the legal voters: So loud and so indecently rude, is the noise made by the distributers of ballots for the different candidates, and such the illiberal reflections and uncandid remarks upon their respective characters, as cannot but excite painful sensations in every delicate mind:—The combined influence of these circumstances, has prevented many an honest and worthy, but infirm, aged, or timid citizen from giving his vote at those meetings. . . .

. . . It is an obvious truth, that the confusion, resulting from the present mode of collecting the votes of the citizens of *Boston,* furnishes to intriguing men an opportunity of affording their favorite candidates illegal support. . . .

66 CANVASSING IN MARYLAND

Maryland appears to have been the first state where "stump speaking" was a common requirement for seeking office. In a letter to William S. Shaw, August 8, 1800, Thomas Boylston Adams, son of President John Adams, describes a Maryland canvass. American Antiquarian Society, *Proceedings*, n.s., XXVII (1917), 120-21.

The Supreme Court are waiting for the Honorable Judge [Samuel] Chase, who is said to be too much engaged in Electioneering, to be able to attend. He is the only man in Maryland perhaps, able to cope with [John Francis] Mercer at, what they call, a Canvass. These are always held, in different parts of the State of Maryland, and generally in the Southern States, as

I am told, when there is known to be a great concourse of people—at a horse race—a cock-fight—or a Methodist quarterly meeting. Here, the Candidates for political honors or preferment, assemble with their partizans—they mount the Rostrum, made out of an empty barrel or hogshead, Harrangue the Sovereign people—praise and recommend themselves at the expence of their adversary's character and pretentions. Such was the mode pursued lately at Anapolis-Elk Ridge, and elsewhere. Col. Mercer, who is a Sovereign Demogague—a fluent and audacious Speaker and a deadly Jacobin—is running as a member of Assembly. Mr. [Philip Barton] Key, whose talents and acquisitions are surpassed by few men in this Country and whose reputation as an Orator is very eminent—is also a Candidate, but in a different district. These Gentlemen met upon the same ground at Anapolis, and canvassed for votes. Key was at home, Mercer was in some measure a stranger, but the contrast between the effect of the two Speakers on the Audience, was very striking. Key triumphed and Mercer slunk away. But at the next place of meeting Mercer played the perfect Buffoon to the singular entertainment of the Sovereign assembly. He laughed—he cried—he stormed by turns, by turns he was placid, "as the smooth surface of a Summer Sea." He abused and vilified President Adam's administration and extolled the virtues of General Washington and Mr. Jefferson. . . .

67 ELECTIONEERING IN SOUTH CAROLINA

Edward Hooker, a Connecticut-born graduate of Yale visiting in western South Carolina, found electioneering practices there surprisingly open and direct. He recorded what seemed to him to be unusual campaign activities in his diary. American Historical Association, *Annual Report, 1896,* I, 896-97, 900-901.

Sun. Sept. 21, [1806] . . . During the service a little event happened, such as I am fond of noting, as exhibiting traits in the manners and character of the people. Two candidates for public favor who were out on an electioneering tour, came into the church attended by two or three others. One was Col. Alston of whom I had heard much in these parts, and who was exerting all his energies to get a seat in Congress: the other was a kind of understrapper to him by the name of Toliver, who was so modest as not to ask for any thing higher than a seat in the State legislature. They were returning from a Barbacue which Alston had yesterday given to the people on twelve-mile-Creek, and it having been last night announced that he would attend church here the expectation of the mountaineers was of course excited: for of the various candidates, he was one in whose favor they were considerably prejudiced. When he came in, all was attention. Men, women and children gazed as at some strange sight. From the Colonel's demeanor, a superficial observer would suppose he really came thither to worship God: but an adept in the science of human nature, would (if a Yankey) be apt to *guess* that he came to worship the people. He seemed to pay the strictest attention to the preacher, and to join fervently in the prayers; and after the hymn was read, he rose from his seat and joined in the singing; at which almost every other man in the house also rose, with an obsequiousness that disgusted me. . . . A curious farce was played at the Church door after meeting. The candidates had stationed themselves conveniently, and were now very busy in saluting every man in the crowd, taking care to call by name as many as possible, and putting themselves on the terms of old acquaintance. Col. Alston was perfect master of the art, and played his game with so much adroitness as almost to persuade one that nobody could have a more cordial attachment to him, or feel a greater interest in his welfare:—but Toliver was much more awkward: and being necessitated to struggle against a more than ordinary share of clownish rusticity, he in attempting to be polite made most blundering work of it. Col. Alston has seen Mr. Lilly formerly and was now quite exuberant in his attentions to him. Myself also he pretended to have seen at Cambridge—was overjoyed to meet with me now etc. etc. He might have seen me—perhaps passing in the street—or in some other situation; but confident I am that he never spoke to me—nor do I recollect ever hearing of such a man till within a short time. I presume it was merely a part of his electioneering system—or in plain terms a downright lie. His whole demeanor however was marked by such easy civility, as to gain the good will of all. He pressingly invited us to extend our journey into the District of Greenville, and to make his house our home for a few days. . . .

Sat. Sept. 27, [*1806*] . . . We arrived at Greenville about 9 and after breakfast, rode to Pickensville 13 miles in company with Col. Alston and a young Mr. Lester. Forded the river Saluda in our way become by this time, a wide, but shallow, stream interrupted by rocks and considerably rapid. Arrived about noon. Quite a public day there. A regiment of cavalry paraded in the woods, made a martial appearance, but there was a coarseness and rusticity about them, characteristic of the country they inhabit. It is said the troops were called out in subserviency to electioneering purposes. Several hundreds of people came together: the houses and streets were thronged. The three candidates for Congress, Alston, Hunter and Earle were present electioneering with all their might—distributing whiskey, giving dinners, talking, and haranguing, their friends at the same time making similar exertions for them. Besides these, there was a number of Candidates for the Assembly. It was a singular scene of noise, blab and confusion. I placed myself on a flight of stairs where I could have a good view of the multitude, and there stood for some time an astonished spectator of a scene, the resemblance of which I had never before witnessed: a scene, ludicrous indeed when superficially observed, but a scene highly alarming, when viewed by one who considers at the same time what inroads are made upon the sacred right of suffrage. Handbills containing accusations of federalism against one, of abuse of public trust against another—of fraudulent speculations against a third—and numerous reports of a slanderous and scurrilous nature were freely circulated. Much drinking, swearing, cursing and threatening—but I saw no fighting. The minds of uninformed people were much agitated—and many well-meaning people were made to believe the national welfare was at stake and would be determined by the issue of this back-woods election. Dr. Hunter conducted with most dignity, or rather with the least indignity on this disgraceful occasion—confining himself to a room in the tavern, and not mixing with the multitude in the street—Alston fought for proselytes and adherents in the street; but took them into the bar-room to treat them but Earle *who loved the people more than any of them,* had his grog bench in the middle of the street and presided over the whiskey jugs himself. Standing behind it like a shop boy behind his counter, and dealing out to any one who would honor him so much as to come up and partake of his *liberality*.

68 A VIRGINIA CANDIDATE RECOUNTS
HIS CAMPAIGN EXPERIENCES

William Brockenbrough refused to treat the voters to grog, but he spent two months campaigning to win election to the Virginia House of Delegates. He discusses his canvass in a letter to Joseph Cabell, June 18, 1801. Cabell Papers, University of Virginia.

I suppose you have seen my Name advertised in the Papers as a Delegate from Essex. This Event has taken place two or three years before I wished it, but both of our former Delegates having declined, a good Opening was left for me to come in. There were four Candidates besides myself, I was therefore obliged to be active. Luckily for me none of my Opponents were very popular. On this account principally, I was elected with considerable Ease. Two months before the Election were almost exclusively appropriated to electioneering. I traversed every part of the County, and became acquainted with almost the whole of the people, with whom before that Time I was wholly unacquainted. I had a good opportunity of observing the state of their Manners, and Sentiments. Many of them I found to be ignorant, brutified and totally indifferent to the Exercise of their most important Rights. The only stimulus with them to that Exercise was through the medium of their palates. Grog, strong Grog was to them of much more Consequence than the giving their Votes for this or that man. These persons I generally neglected, having determined not to gain my Election by such means, and I succeeded, for I believe I did not spend two Dollars during the two Months, in which I canvassed. Some I found to be extremely independent, and intelligent, and it was by the Votes of these men, and the neighborhood Influence which they possessed, that I was elected. Others again, not so bad as the first, although they put on the appearance of Independence, yet possessing it not in Reality, required a great Deal of courting. Many exhibited a very reasonable kind of Jealousy, they required purity in their Delegate, and that he should have the same Interest with themselves. The being a Lawyer was with some a fatal objection, taking it for granted that a Lawyer was interested in multiplying Laws, and in rendering them more complex, and the very Idea that a man was looking out for an office or intended to desert them after a year or two shocked them exceedingly.

69 THOMAS MANN RANDOLPH SEEKS ELECTION IN VIRGINIA

A son-in-law of President Jefferson, Randolph published this campaign appeal in his successful bid for election to Congress in 1803. *To the Freeholders of Albemarle, Amherst and Fluvanna,* broadside, Library of Congress.

On Friday the fourth instant, the Seventh Congress of the United States terminated. Then also expired the power you delegated to your late Representative. . . . Colonel Cabell offers his services to you again. I, also, tender you mine; and stand ready, if you choose to accept them, to employ for you all the faculties, such as they are, which nature gave, or art may have created for me. . . . It has been your long established practice to choose among those who voluntarily offer themselves to your choice. It is not probable you will change that practice now, tho' I hope you will at some future time, take it into your consideration. I therefore place myself in your view, knowing that you will not take from the number you have among you, infinitely preferable to myself, and anxiously wishing that you should have an agent of more youth and health, more patient of literary confinement, and more fond of legislative labour, than your late highly respectable, and otherwise, valuable representative. One of us two by old custom, you must take. It will no doubt be the one, your judgment, without favor, will determine. In making that judgment, your attention will naturally be directed to three positive requisites, and to two other points of comparative character. The absolute requisites are, sound moral principles, true political opinions and feelings, identity of private interests with your own. The points of comparison are, political and general knowledge, and ability to undergo, with effect, literary labours. The impossibility of personal communication with all of you, in the short time between this and the election, which the fear of appearing to take an illiberal advantage of the absence of my competitor has given, compels me to state, here, my pretensions to your approbation and confidence. Not that I am ignorant of the little credit given by the wise, to the declarations men make concerning themselves. No. I approve that caution; I feel the justice and prudence of it. But *I* mean chiefly, to state facts, about which you have time to make enquiry. When it is considered that myself, must necessarily be the subject of an address, on such an occasion my speaking of myself will be excused. On the first requisite, nothing need be said: the morals of both have ever stood and I dare pronounce ever will stand unimpeached, unsuspected. For the second, my near alliance to that man, who, aided by a very few, upheld political liberty, when it had been beaten down in all the world besides, and was fast sinking in this its last retreat, might answer. But I wave the advantage. . . . I call on you, to inform yourselves, in my own neighbourhood, that *I* have always professed those sentiments, and steadily, acted for their support, on every occasion, which the narrow sphere of my agricultural life afforded. To the same source, *I* direct you, to learn the identity of my private interests, with your own. *I* acquaint you, that *I* have no estate but land, (for the most part within your district,) and that species of property which is necessary for its cultivation. That *I* have not one penny of income, but what is annually dug from that land, by the hands of my servants under my own daily superintendance, or is given me voluntarily, by freemen, or that part of the profits of agriculture, due for the soil. *I* have a wife, who was born in the district, and a family of five children, which is settled permanently in it. On all questions then, which relate to burthens on the people, or concern internal tranquility, my interests are the same with yours. I am within the age, which subjects us all to military duties, and shall be yet, for a great many years, if my life continues. I feel myself able to undergo those duties, and *I* pledge my honor to you, that while *I* remain so, *I* will use no advantage *I* possess, or priviledge *I* may obtain, to shun them. My competitor, it is true, has served in the field. That *I* have not, has happened through the good fortune of my country: from that circumstance, therefore, *I* cannot surely, in justice, incur even comparative disqualification. . . . The comparison between us, involved in the two last points, on which *I* have concluded you will examine your candidates, must be made, upon other information, than their own assertions or promises. Here my competitor has a great advantage over me. He has served eight years in Congress. You can by enquiry, ascertain the degree of activity he has displayed, the amount of the exertions his mind has made, during that service; and your concern for your own interests will impel you to make that enquiry. You can ask and be informed, which of the measures you approve, were prompted or forwarded by him; what aid he gave in counteracting the mischievous propositions and attempts, you know have been made, and rejoice have been defeated. Thus you can weigh, with sufficient precision, his knowledge and his powers; and no doubt you will weigh them, since those of another are offered for your choice. But of that other, indeed, you have not those sure means of forming a judgment. I have never yet been in public life. I have followed no calling but that of practical agriculture. I have had no very rare or splendid advantages, in early education. What powers I may have are derived from nature, or formed by private discipline. What knowledge I may possess, must have been chiefly acquired by silent reflection, in the midst of labors and cares, such as daily occupy all of you. You will not surely depreciate those means, the only ones yourselves possess. You must be conscious, I am satisfied, that by such reflection, a deep insight into the primary principles of all human knowledge, arts, and affairs, can be obtained, and the clue seized, which leads, with certainty, to sound judgment and right conduct, in all ordinary agencies, or trusts, the people may think proper to give, to those disposed for exertion in their service. It is the inestimable distinction, the glorious priviledge of our country, that every citizen may ask promotion, of the people, without danger of ridicule to himself, if he be otherwise above it; and if he be found likely to be useful, may obtain it without disgrace to the nation. The priviledge you must honor, tho' the promotion may, perhaps in my case, be refused. The refusal shall not damp my desire to serve you.

70   A CALL FOR PARTY LOYALTY

In this official party circular of Delaware Jeffersonians can be seen the theme of party loyalty repeatedly emphasized in party literature throughout the country. Broadside, September 14, 1805, Library of Congress.

To the Democratic Republican Hundred Committees, of the Respective Hundreds of Newcastle County

IN appealing, on the approaching General Election, to the undiminished zeal and unwearied perseverance of the Democratic Republican Citizens of Newcastle County, through their regular organs, the Hundred Committees;—The Corresponding Committee for the County, feel all the confidence inspired by a thorough knowledge of their firmness and devotion to the general interest. Each revolving year gives rise to new motives for exertion, as our Political Adversaries are perpetually endeavouring to overthrow the fabric that has been reared on the foundation of the genuine principles of Democracy:—To defend and preserve the system, would seem to require as much, if not more activity and attention than to establish it;—very fortunately our Citizens possess a pride of character and a tenacious adherence to measures deliberately adopted, especially when approved by experience, that prepares them to resist with energy every attempt at improper innovation. To exclude from office under our Governments those, whose political principles are considered inimical to Republican Institutions, is deemed a primary duty—and the exercise of the Elective Franchise is the only legitimate mode of performing that duty. Men who are too indolent to assert, or who for other causes do not duly appreciate the right of self-government scarcely deserve to be free—Come forward then Republican Friends, bring with you your less active neighbours to the General Election on the first Tuesday in October next, and shew to the world, by a temperate, manly, and determined exercise of the right of suffrage, that you merit its possession to the fullest extent:—A Representative to Congress for this state is to be chosen on that day, and DAVID HALL is the Candidate selected for the office by the Democratic Republican Conferees on the occasion of their late meeting at the town of Dover. The Conferees from Newcastle County were chosen by the people themselves, and made the selection, we firmly believe, with a disinterested view to the general good. In deliberately weighing the act, we are decidedly of opinion, that it is the duty as well as policy of every Democratic Citizen to afford it his utmost support. That each individual should be gratified with the selection for office of the man he most approves, is not to be expected; as much, if not more difference of opinion, existing among men with respect to fitness for office than almost on any other subject;—hence the necessity of adopting a method by which unanimity may be produced. The mode resorted to on this occasion (choosing Representatives to express the will of the people) conforms to the soundest principle of Democracy;—and the first and most important tenet in its creed—*that the will of the majority should govern*—engages *the people* to unite and give their suffrages to the Candidate who has been selected, not by the majority solely, but by the unanimous voice of their Representatives;—this must not only be a persuasive but an imperative argument with Republican Citizens, who, by these measures, have attained the vantage ground of political ascendancy, and by persevering in them, can alone hope to retain their elevated station. It is sincerely believed by the Corresponding Committee, that David Hall is as unexceptionable a Candidate as could perhaps have been selected, and will undoubtedly unite in his favour more suffrages in Kent and Sussex than any person that could have been obtained from this County. The County Nomination of Candidates also meets our fullest approbation.—Republicans, we earnestly solicit you cordially to co-operate at the ensuing Election by your union and exertion.

. . . Let us then fellow-citizens, as a pledge of our success, commence immediate, active and energetic operations to promote the election of David Hall, the Democratic candidate for Representative to Congress, *as highly worthy to be supported for that important trust—and the Republican Ticket generally:*—The more surely to effect these objects, we recommend to you to meet together on the 25th of this month in your respective Hundreds, and concert and determine on the general plan of operation, and the best means of bringing the people forward to the Election.

G. READ, *President of the Democratic Republican corresponding committee for Newcastle County*

RICHARD C. DALE, *Secretary*
Newcastle, September 14th, 1805

71   TREATING KENTUCKY VOTERS

This unusually candid contemporary commentary on treating and other electioneering practices was published in a campaign circular by Robert H. Grayson, Mason County, June 5, 1806. Grayson was unsuccessful in his bid for election to Congress. Broadside, Filson Club.

I have been told by some, (and for the honor of the district the number was but small) that I was wrong in condemning the practice of treating and feasting for votes, a practice, which I think every independent voter will condemn, and which however it may be smoothed over is the worst kind of corruption in elections, as the motives of those who adopt it, cannot always be discovered. If *one single vote* is obtained by any thing of this kind, the election cannot be said to be a *fair* expression of the public will. Altho I am no prophet, I think I may venture to predict from the example of other nations, that if ever we loose our liberties, it will be by the people, first suffering intrigue and corruption to creep into their elections, by the combinations of influential men among us, or by the voters loosing their virtue. It is remarkable that those who have introduced large expences into elections, have generally said that they were friends to the poor, although they have been the first to desert them, when their ends are obtained. The poorest part of our citizens (if indeed there is truly a poor man among us) will see, that although we are now rich in liberty, that by incourageing expences and corruption in elections, in time a system of things will take place, which will effectually exclude them from offices of honor under our government, however they may be entitled to them from their merit. Although I may loose some votes by condemning a practice, which indirectly tends to sap the foundation of our liberties and morality, yet a republican who acts upon principle, ought always to express freely his sentiments upon subjects which may be injurious to the public.

It is a misfortune, sir, for this country, that electioneering (as it is called) has been so compleatly reduced to a science, as with us. Candidates are in the habit of making appeals to the passions and prejudices, not the reason of the voter. Duplicity, flattery and the most shameful political and religious hypocricy are frequently resorted to. To prevent a *fair expression* of the public voice, they frequently act over the whole comedy of tricks and maneuvres, and he who plays his part the best is praised for his *address*. Cameleon like, you see them changing colors, and in order to please, they are saints and sinners by turns, as occasion may require. Treating some of the voters, in open violation of the laws of our country, is practised under pretence of *sociability*. The whole dictionary of insipid jokes is consulted and these jokes dealt out with great profusion upon all occasions and in all companies, as if men were to be sent to Congress, or to the assembly, to act the part of Buffoons or jesters. Intemperance, it seems, is not always an improper qualification for a candidate. A pack of cards, a keg of whisky, and a game cock, have on some occasions (it is said) been a good electioneering apparatus, for a man, who if elected, was to assist in making laws for a nation. But this is not all, the candidate according to the present mode of electioneering, if he wishes to succeed, must, for at least a year before the election, totally neglect his private affairs, however inconvenient it may be to him, and instead of having that necessary time for preparing himself, to discharge properly the trust reposed in him by the people, if elected, he has perpetually to take the rounds, through the district with the velocity of a race rider. If he does not do this, there are not wanting men to accuse him of neglect and pride. These measures to obtain an election cannot long be countenanced. They are pursued in no other state in the Union. The people will open their eyes, and ask why men adopt these extraordinary means to obtain success if they had nothing in view but the good of their country?

VIII PARTY CAMPAIGN APPEALS

Through newspapers, handbills, leaflets, circular and private letters, and word of mouth, active party workers sought to put their views and programs before the voters. While the presidential election of 1796 had been dominated by issues centering on the characters and principles of the two leading contestants, John Adams and Thomas Jefferson, by 1800 the Jeffersonian Republicans presented the electorate with what amounted to a party platform, and the Federalists offered reasoned defenses of their party record. The voters were thus presented with meaningful alternatives, although these were frequently engulfed by emotion-charged appeals to passions, fears, and interests. Candidates were eulogized and abused; issues were distorted and ignored. There were appeals to economic interests, to religious feelings, and to state and regional attachments. Yet, despite the provoking of passions and prejudices and the inflamed language of partisan conflict, considerable attention was focused on the performance of parties: the Federalist record under Adams and the Republican record under Jefferson.

Although their phraseology marks them as being of an earlier era, the campaign appeals common in the young Republic display many techniques which subsequent party strategists have repeatedly employed. Special emphasis on taxes and governmental expenses is particularly noticeable. There was also an effort made by Republicans to transfer Jefferson's mantle of popularity to Madison, suggesting a practice that has become commonplace in American politics.

72 A REPUBLICAN CAMPAIGN SHEET
CONTRASTS ADAMS AND JEFFERSON

This address, October 3, 1796, was distributed by Pennsylvania Republicans during the presidential election of 1796. Broadside, Historical Society of Pennsylvania.

FELLOW CITIZENS!

The first concern of Freeman, calls you forth into action.—Pennsylvania was never yet found wanting when Liberty was at stake; she cannot then be indifferent when the question is, *Who shall be President of the United States?* The citizen who now holds the office of President, has publicly made known to his fellow citizens that he declines to serve in it again. Two candidates are offered to your choice, as his successor; THOMAS JEFFERSON of Virginia, and JOHN ADAMS of New England.—No other candidate is proposed, you cannot therefore mistake between them. THOMAS JEFFERSON is the man who was your late Secretary of State, and Minister of the United States to the French nation; JOHN ADAMS is the man who is now Vice President of the United States, and was late the Minister to the king of Great Britain.—THOMAS JEFFERSON is a firm REPUBLICAN, —JOHN ADAMS is an avowed MONARCHIST. . . .

Thomas Jefferson first drew the declaration of American independence; —he first framed the sacred political sentence that all men are *born* equal. *John Adams* says this is all a farce and a falsehood; that some men should be born Kings, and some should be born Nobles. Which of these, freemen of Pennsylvania, will you have for your President? Will you, by your votes, contribute to make the avowed friend of monarchy, President?—or will you, by neglectfully staying at home, permit others to saddle you with Political Slavery? *Adams* has Sons who might aim to succeed their father; *Jefferson,* like Washington, has no Son. *Adams* is a fond admirer of the British Constitution, and says it is the first wonder of the world. *Jefferson* likes better our Federal Constitution, and thinks the British full of deformity, corruption and wickedness. Once more, fellow citizens! Choose ye between those two, which you will have for President, *Jefferson* or *Adams*. Remember Friday the fourth of November; attend your elections on that day; put in your tickets for fifteen good REPUBLICANS, and let the watch word be LIBERTY and INDEPENDENCE!

73 A VIRGINIA REPUBLICAN URGES, "BRING OUR ARGUMENTS HOME TO THEIR FEELINGS"

Meriwether Jones to Creed Taylor, April 9, 1799, Creed Taylor Papers, University of Virginia.

I hope my friend in your conversations with the people, you frequently recur to governmental expenses:—it is an ample field and one on which the people ought to be well informed. 'Tis in vain in the present temper of the United States to talk of *principle;* from that there has been considerable defection: we ought therefore to bring our arguments home to their feelings. I am sorry to speak so ill of the *sovereign people,* but they have really become very mercenary, and of consequence opposed to war expenses. Let *peace* and *economy* then be our constant theme, and exhibit to them fair statements of expenditures.

74 A FEDERALIST LEADER ADVISES, "SOUND THE TOCSIN ABOUT JEFFERSON"

Fisher Ames to Oliver Wolcott, June 12, 1800. George Gibbs, *Memoirs of the Administrations of Washington and John Adams, edited from the Papers of Oliver Wolcott* (New York: 1846), II, 368-70.

. . . All the influence of office, of popular prejudices, and habits, and all the effect of the arts of our political rivals are manifest at this moment, and the division of the federal people, and the augmented spirit and force of the antis are evils scarcely to be avoided. My thoughts are, that as the unanimous vote of Massachusetts must be had, the plain truth, which in other moments can alone work miracles to save, would now operate to divide us. That, instead of analyzing the measures of the man who has thus brought the cause into jeopardy, you must sound the tocsin about Jefferson; that the hopes and fears of the citizens are the only source of influence, and surely we have enough to fear from Jefferson; by thus continually sounding our just alarms we remain united with the people, instead of separated from them, and losing at least a part of our influence. . . . Why not then, without delay, begin a series of papers to prove the dreadful evils to be apprehended from a Jacobin President. . . . The men, the means, the end of such a government as Jefferson must, *nolens volens,* prefer, will soon ensure war with Great Britain, a Cisalpine alliance with France, plunder and anarchy.

Such ideas exhibited with vivacity and force, would arouse the public, if the sleep of death be not already upon us.

75 A FEDERALIST PICTURE OF THE CONSEQUENCES OF THE ELECTION OF JEFFERSON

A Short Address to the Voters of Delaware, Kent County, September 21, 1800, signed "A Christian Federalist." Pamphlet, Library of Congress.

The importance of the approaching election does not appear to be sufficiently felt, by those on whom the cause of *Federalism* depends. They seem not to perceive that great national interests are at stake, as well as those essential principles, on which the immediate peace and security of society, and also the hopes of future happiness rest.

Can serious and reflecting men look about them and doubt, that if Jefferson is elected, and the Jacobins get into authority, that those morals which protect our lives from the knife of the assassin—which guard the chastity of our wives and daughters from seduction and violence—defend our property from plunder and devastation, and shield our religion from contempt and profanation, will not be trampled upon and exploded. Men are the same in their natures in different countries and at different times. Operated upon by the same causes, they are impelled in the same courses. A Frenchman bred from early infancy, and habituated to the customs of this country, would resemble in temper and manners, an American; under like circumstances, a similar effect would be produced on an American in France.

Under a regular government, we have seen the French the most polite, polished and humane people in Europe. We have seen them without a government, more ferocious than savages, more bloody than tygers, more impious than demons. Recall the scene of the revolution for a moment. . . . You have seen a rich flourishing and happy nation become a scene of bloodshed, rapine and devastation, and deluged with all the crimes and miseries which spring from the ungoverned passion of wicked men.

These things we at first saw with astonishment and horror; but their continuance rendering them familiar, we at last viewed them with simple apathy. Will you pause, Fellow-Citizens, and enquire what produced those afflicting and wonderful events in France, and will you then ask do causes exist in this country capable of producing the same effect? In France, it was the suffering men of false and wicked principles to get into power, *men who taught that there was no God—no Saviour—no future rewards and punishments, but that death was an eternal sleep*—Men who could publicly set up a strumpet decorated in the garments of a religious form, and in the face of a people of a great capital, under the name of the goddess of Reason, worship her as the image of the only true Supreme Being. Such men easily believed, that crimes were mere inventions of priestcraft, and that when they had power they possessed the right of gratifying their ambition, or of indulging their passions at the expense of torrents of blood, and the indiscriminate miseries of thousands of their fellow creatures. I will not disgust you with an enumeration of the catalogues of crimes, which cast so black a mantle over the licentious periods of the French revolution. And now my fellow citizens do you not believe that there are men in the United States, as unprincipled and profligate as any who existed in France? In France, Danton, Marat, and Robespierre, were flaming patriots—staunch democrats, and great sticklers for the rights of man. *Such was the mask they wore,* and do you not see that mask, which even French impudence is at present ashamed to wear, now covering the hypocrisy of our pretended republicans? Trace the history of the furious and bloody demagogues of the revolution, and then remark the correspondence with the acts of demagogues at home. By the same affected attachment to the rights and interests of the people, they endeavour to gain their affections and confidence, in order to use them as the instruments of their ambition. Let these men get into power, put the reins of government into their hands, and what security have you against the occurrence of the scenes which have rendered France a cemetery, and moistened her soil with the tears and blood of her inhabitants? . . .

Remember that the reign of anarchy may create more evil in a year, than the order of government can eradicate in a century. What is it that your modern philosophers hold sacred in society? The name of religion is odious to them, and in order to extinguish the remembrance of the sabbath, the day of worship, they have converted the week into the decade, and they adopted generally the principle which the Spartans confined to theft —that a man commits no crime unless he is detected.

This, my fellow-citizens, is a true but imperfect view of the grounds of our political disputes and parties. Our government is as free as it is capable of being—the country as happy as a government can make it. What more do you want? Will you grasp at a shadow, and lose the substance?

When they talk of a violation of the constitution, is there a man among you who can say he *ever saw it or felt it;* will you believe such things before *you see* or *feel them?* Will you be governed by your *own eyes and feelings,* or *those of other people?* Others have an interest to deceive you; you have

none to deceive yourselves. Trust yourselves, therefore, before others.—
What is all the cry about republicanism? Do any of you know a man who
is an enemy to republicanism? Did you hear him say so? Or what did you
see him do which would lead to such an opinion? This is the 12th year of
our government, and it has been in the same hands, and is it not as free
and republican as it was the first year? If the *Jeffersonites* wish more
republicanism, what must it consist in? Not in the freedom of equal laws,
which is true republicanism; but in the licentiousness of anarchy, which in
fact is the worst of tyranny. Let me press this question upon you, are not
the offices of the government open to all, and do not the laws rest equally
on the shoulders of all?

This they say is not republicanism; and indeed, fellow-citizens, it is not
what they mean by republicanism. The short system of their republicanism
is the possession of all power, by the new sect of Philosophers; and in the
extermination of all principle, which can bridle their passion in the enjoyment of it. A feeling heart which perceives an honest man, deluded by the
hypocritical noise about republicanism, must weep over the frailty of human
nature, so dangerous to its interest and peace. . . .

76 "THE GRAND QUESTION STATED"

A notice repeatedly printed in the Federalist *Gazette of the United
States* (Philadelphia) during September, 1800, pointed up a key election issue.

THE GRAND QUESTION STATED

At the present solemn and momentous epoch, the only question to be
asked by every American, laying his hand on his heart is "shall I continue
in allegiance to

GOD—AND A RELIGIOUS PRESIDENT;
Or impiously declare for
JEFFERSON—AND NO GOD!!!"

77 VIRGINIA FEDERALISTS OPPOSE CHANGE

A reasoned argument against change was issued by the Federalist state
committee in Virginia. *An Address, To the Voters for Electors of President and Vice President of the United States, in the State of Virginia,*
Richmond, May 26, 1800, signed by William Austin, secretary. Broadside, Library of Congress.

The reasons we have to be satisfied with our present government, it would be long, and we hope unnecessary, to detail. The uncorrupted feelings of every American should make it unnecessary; nor need he learn from foreigners the increasing prosperity of our happy country, while the severest calamity afflicts almost the whole of the civilized world, and has nearly ruined the fairest portion of it. To the adoption of our constitution, to the sage maxims of administration established by the immortal WASHINGTON, and steadily pursued by his virtuous successor, may fairly be ascribed our present prosperous situation. The man who calmly contemplates, and can wish to change it, may be compared to the great enemy of mankind surveying maliciously the first abodes of happiness and peace.

But, an unvarying course of prosperity, like the even tenor of health, makes no impression; while we betray a quick sensibility to the slightest misfortune or pain. We forget that our government has preserved us from two impending wars, the foundation of which was laid before its existance, with the two most powerful nations of the world, armed to the full extent of their powers; and that, without any sacrifice of the national interest, or of the national honor. We forget that we have been preserved from a close alliance with either of those nations, which would have been the worst, and the most inevitable, consequences of a war with the other; and that we remain, if we will, completely free and independent. But the fleet, the army, the taxes, all the little evils which were necessary to the attainment of these great and invaluable objects, make a strong impression, and are attributed as crimes to the government.

In the eager desire of change, even the meaning of language is perverted, in order to justify it. Thus the free, peaceful, and flourishing condition of the United States, under the guidance of WASHINGTON, the father of his country, is called "the calm of despotism." (See letter to Mazzei, ascribed to Mr. Jefferson.) * Shall we then embark, with this writer, on "the tempestuous sea of liberty?" When tired of the voyage, vainly may we strive to regain our present peaceful haven. We must endure the unceasing storms, and deeply drink the bloody waves, and find no refuge at last, but in the calm of real despotism. Let us be content to take a lesson, on this head, from the French republic, rather than from our own experience.

*Jefferson to Philip Mazzei, April 24, 1796, Ford, ed., *Writings of Thomas Jefferson,* VII, 75-76. A version of the letter was published in the New York *Minerva,* May 14, 1797.

78 REPUBLICANS ATTACK THE RECORD
OF THE ADAMS ADMINISTRATION

This attack on the Federalist record was adopted by "Deputies from the several republican county-meetings" in New Jersey, September 30, 1800, and published in an address *To the People of New-Jersey.* Broadside, Historical Society of Pennsylvania.

. . . We are called upon to elect a chief magistrate of this extensive country; on this election depends the future happiness of America. When freed from foreign oppression, and privileged to choose our own rulers, it was presumed that the people of America would remain the peaceable cultivators of their fields, uninfluenced by the policies of European courts, and regardless of their destinies. But the experience of a few years has removed the pleasing delusion.

Our agriculture is oppressed by taxation.

Our manufactures are superceded by British productions.

Our commerce subjected to the spoliations of foreign cruisers: and

Our national councils agitated by a faction, declared to be formed by England. . . .

We are paying an enormous tribute to the petty tyrant of Algiers.

We have had an Alien and still have a Sedition law; by which many citizens have been deprived of their rights, and native Americans consigned to loathsome prisons for exercising the constitutional right of public enquiry.

We are struggling under a direct tax, with heavy imposts; raising money on loan at *Eight* per cent.—And our expenditures are encreasing, while our national debt is accumulating.

We have supported an army in time of peace, while our militia is neglected. The latter, said our beloved *Washington,* "is the natural defense of a country."

We have an expensive and ineffectual navy, to support the interest of foreign merchants at the sacrifice of naval, agricultural, and mechanical interests.

We have a variety of stock-jobbing acts which have given birth to a system of speculation, fraud, and bankruptcy.

We have witnessed the effects of presidential patronage, we have seen with regret, *British subjects* raised to posts of honor and profit, to the exclusion of *honest Americans,* who braved the perils of a long and bloody war.

We have seen old tories, the enemies of our revolution, recommended as the guardians of our country.

We have seen——but time is not sufficient, to recapitulate the abuses of our constitution.—This catalogue contains only a *few* facts—facts serious in themselves, woefully notorious, and in principle demanding the strictest scrutiny. . . .

79 THE PHILADELPHIA *Aurora* PUBLISHES THE REPUBLICAN PLATFORM

The term *platform* was not in use in 1800, nor was there any official party declaration of principles, but Jefferson and other party leaders clearly outlined what amounted to a platform, and here the Republican press printed a version of the party's program. *Aurora,* October 14, 1800.

ATTENTION
Citizens of Philadelphia
Take Your Choice

FEDERAL Things As They Have Been	REPUBLICAN Things As They Will Be
1. The principles and patriots of the *Revolution* condemned and stigmatized.	1. The Principles of the *Revolution* restored; its Patriots honored and beloved.
2. *Republicanism,* a badge for persecution, and federalism a mask for monarchy.	2. *Republicanism* proved to mean something, and Federalism found to mean nothing.
3. The *Nation* in arms without a foe, and divided without a cause.	3. The *Nation* at peace with the world, and united in itself.
4. *Federalists* graduating a scale of *"hatred and animosity,"* for the benefit of the people; and aiming *"a few bold strokes"* at political opposition, for the benefit of themselves.	4. *Republicanism* allaying the fever of domestic feuds, and subduing the opposition by the force of reason and rectitude.
5. The reign of terror created by false alarms, to promote domestic feud and foreign war.	5. Unity, peace, and concord produced by republican measures and equal laws.
6. Systems of rapine, fraud, and plunder by public defaulters under countenance of public servants.	6. Public plunderers and defaulters called to strict account, and public servants compelled to do their duty.

7. Priests and Judges incorporated with the Government for political purposes, and equally polluting the holy altars of religion, and the seats of Justice.

7. Good government without the aid of priestcraft, or religious politics, and Justice administered without political intolerance.

8. Increase of Public Debt
   Additional Taxes
   Further Loans
   New Excises
   Higher Public Salaries, and
   Wasteful Expenditure of public money.

8. Decrease of Public Debt
   Reduced Taxes
   No Loans
   No Excises
   Reduced Public Salaries, and a system of economy and care of the public money.

9. Quixotish embassies to the Turks, the Russians, Prussians, and Portuguese, for Quixotish purposes of holding the balance of Europe.

9. The republican maxim of our departed Washington, "Not to intermeddle with European politics."

10. A Sedition Law to protect corrupt magistrates and public defaulters.

10. The Liberty of the Press, and free enquiry into public character, and our constitutional charter.

11. An established church, a religious test, and an order of Priesthood.

11. Religious liberty, the rights of conscience, no priesthood, truth and Jefferson.

80   FEDERALISTS ATTACK THE JEFFERSONIAN RECORD

With the reversal of the party situation brought about by the Republican victory in 1800, the Federalists were soon challenging the Jeffersonian performance, as Republicans had earlier attacked the Federalist record. *Address of the Federal Republican Committee of Kent County, to the Electors of the Same* [Kent County, Maryland, 1803], signed by John Clarke, chairman. Broadside, Library of Congress.

. . . The ensuing General Election, from the particular situation of public affairs, is extremely important. The Government of the United States, both Executive and Legislative, is committed to Mr. Jefferson and *his friends.* His wishes, no doubt, will be obsequiously gratified at the next meeting of Congress; and, therefore, on the part of the several States every possible degree of vigilance should be used.

Mr. Jefferson has made a treaty with Bonaparte, the First Consul of

France, for the purchase of Louisiana, at the price of Fifteen Millions of Dollars—This sum must be discharged by the United States; our proportion of this debt to be paid in some way, will be above two hundred thousand dollars. Without further information upon this subject, we will not venture absolutely to condemn this treaty; but we think this is a sufficient cause to excite the utmost watchfulness on the part of the people. If we elect *Mr. Jefferson's friends* into the Legislature, we are morally certain they will approve his measures be they ever so ruinous in their consequences. The possession of this extensive Territory does not seem to comport with the true interest of the United States.—Our population is already too much diffused, and by still enlarging our bounds we actually weaken the nation. By our treaty with Spain, we had a right to the navigation of the Mississippi, and were entitled to deposit our goods at New-Orleans. The Spaniards deprived us of this place of deposit; and our true policy only required the regaining it—instead of which, we have acquired a distant useless country, and are saddled with the enormous sum of fifteen millions of dollars. Thus our public debt is accumulating; and new taxes upon our houses, lands and upon the necessaries of life, must be resorted to, to meet this new demand.

Another source of distrust arises from a grant made by Congress at their last Session to Mr. Jefferson of two millions of dollars, for foreign intercourse. This sum is greater by a million and a half of dollars than was ever granted under the administration of General Washington or Mr. Adams. Thus, at one leap, as soon as Mr. Jefferson and *his friends* obtained full possession of the government, they exceeded in this article the former administrations by the enormous sum of one million five hundred thousand dollars, and without specifying any particular time in which this unreasonable allowance is to be accounted for. . . .

. . . After the experiment of two years, from what burthen, from what expence have we been relieved? It is true the taxes on stills, pleasurable carriages, loaf sugar, and some other superfluities, have been repealed, but was the tax on whiskey or brandy a burthen? Was the tax imposed on carriages of pleasure a burthen on the people? Was the duty paid on loaf sugar a burthen on the people? The answer to these questions must be in the negative. They were none of them burthens; they were real benefits to the great body of the people, for they were paid by the wealthy, and not by the poor or labouring part of the community. On the other hand are not the taxes on coffee, on molasses, on brown sugar, and on salt, real burthens, and oppressive impositions on the mass of the nation? These articles constitute the real necessaries of life; no poor man can, or does live without them, and yet he is taxed for what is absolutely requisite to his existence, when the superfluous enjoyments of the rich are exempted from contribution.

Thus we find Mr. Jefferson's administration has produced an increase of our public debt 15,000,000 of dollars; a grant to him of 2,000,000 more without limiting any time of account; a repeal of the taxes on luxuries, and a continuance of the duties on the necessaries of life.

The impenetrable veil of secrecy, which Mr. Jefferson and *his friends* have thrown over their management of public affairs, partaking much of regal haughtiness, exhibits strong proof of the lordly temper of the present administration, and of the real contempt in which they hold their constituents. The whole progress of the Louisiana business, has been involved in mystery. It commenced in an obscure communication to congress, was conducted with closed doors, and has ended in a treaty involving us in a new debt to the amount of 15,000,000 of dollars—Even the law granting 2,000,000 was passed in secret, and no one circumstance relative to this extensive and unspecified appropriation of public treasure has been suffered to transpire. Thus we see that the present administration conceals from the knowledge of the people, their most momentous concerns, and will not suffer them to judge of the propriety of public measures. Without full information of the conduct of our Representatives, we are deprived of the power of rightly exercising one of our most important and valuable privileges; that is of choosing our legislators. If they misbehave we can, and ought to remove them; but if they conceal those measures which most essentially affect our rights, and our property, how can we form a correct judgment of their conduct. The fact itself is full proof that they ought not to be trusted; and neither ought those who sanction such unjustifiable proceedings to be elected. . . .

81   REPUBLICANS DEFEND THE JEFFERSONIAN RECORD

To the Democratic Republican Electors, of the State of Pennsylvania [1804]. Broadside, Library of Congress.

The choice of Electors of the President and Vice-President, is to be made on Friday, the 2d of November. . . . Let nothing make us backward, inactive, cold or divided in this all important case. The Tree of Liberty will take deep root, grow high, spread wide and be well matured under Jefferson and Clinton in the next four years. To true democrats no argument is necessary on this occasion, yet time admits us to observe, that in the administration of Jefferson the excises and direct tax have been repealed, and with them numerous offices have been abolished. Our finances have been entrusted to a Pennsylvanian. The Mississippi and every opportunity to trade on its banks and from its mouth have been secured to us. The Indians have been kept in peace, 'til we have got 30,000 militia in our own western counties. The post-roads have been extended. Religious Liberty remains *the favourite fostered plant* in the Garden of Freedom. The militia has been nursed and rival aristocratic *"volunteers"* have been discouraged. Regular troops have been kept within proper limits by republican caution and prudence. No new treaty of *tribute* has been made with Algerine pirates. There have been no quarrels in our cabinet councils, but we have quietly taken an old whig soldier (Clinton) for Vice-President instead of one whose conduct we could not possibly approve. The judiciary power of the United States is replaced on the footing it stood on when Washington and Jefferson were together in our national administration, and the judges seem competent to do all the business. The President has no more allowance in 1804 than the President had in 1789, though our nation, over which he presides, is nearly twice as numerous. We have been kept from wars of ambition and plunder, which are real murders *upon the scale of thousands*. We have even avoided defensive war by a wise and economical policy. No foreign power has been made resentful, by insulting and impolitic speeches of the President. Manufactures from grain and perishable fruit, also from wood, iron, leather, etc. have been relieved from excises of nearly a million of dollars a year. Levees and other matters of parade have been abolished. The expences of our Army and Navy and Indian affairs have been made easier by procuring supplies more and more from our manufacturers. The naturalization law has been altered from the extreme term of fourteen years to a term nine years shorter, according to the time fixed in the administration of Washington. The body of monarchists in the country has been deprived of much of its support, because many federalists disgusted with their hereditary principles, have ceased to oppose the national administration, whose conduct they confess is favorable to public prosperity.

82 A FEDERALIST VIEW OF EIGHT YEARS
UNDER JEFFERSON

Hartford *Connecticut Courant*, April 6, 1808.

No election since the establishment of our federal government, has been as interesting in many points of view as the present. The Jeffersonian administration, have led us blindfold into the most perilous situation—they have brought us to the brink of ruin, by their weak, or worse than weak measures—they have destroyed our trade, beggared our seamen, cut off the farmer from his market, and the mechanic from his trade—our merchants are ruined because their business is broken up, credit is annihilated—and to crown the whole, we are madly rushing into a destructive war with Great-Britain, because Mr. Jefferson and Mr. Madison insist upon it that they will protect deserters from British vessels. All these concurring evils, have caused a great and increasing alarm in the country, and all classes and parties are eagerly enquiring into the causes of our national troubles. Alas! they enquire in vain. We have suffered ourselves to be led by the nose tamely and submissively, apparently satisfied with ruin, if we are only ruined by Mr. Jefferson. He keeps all to himself, and we are allowed to ask no questions—or if we ask, we are denied all answer. In order to shew that we are the friends of free and unmolested trade, foes to useless embargoes, and opposers of war, let the

FARMER,

look at his produce on hand perishing for want of a market.—Let the

MECHANIC,

thrown out of his trade for the want of that employment, which in former times gave him and his family a comfortable living.—Let the

SEAMAN,

who has been for months lounging about the wharves, without employment, and without wages—let the

DAY-LABOURER,

whose spade and axe have been thrown by as useless—and let

ALL CLASSES

of men, unite their suffrages to elect those men to office, who will exert their best talents to save our sinking country.

83 THE REPUBLICAN CENTRAL COMMITTEE OF MASSACHUSETTS ACCUSES THE FEDERALISTS OF APPEALS TO PASSIONS AND PREJUDICES

"To the Electors of Massachusetts," Boston *Democrat*, March 26, 1808, and Boston *Independent Chronicle*, March 28, 1808.

The electioneering exertions and intrigues of the Federalists call for vigilance on the part of the Republicans.

From year to year, it has been the federal practice upon the approach of an important election, to operate on the public mind, by spreading some popular alarm. At one time *Religion* was in danger. The electors were told, with affected concern, that if the Republicans should succeed, our churches would be demolished, our bibles burned, and the clergy massacred. When the public credulity could no longer be influenced by that topic, the *Constitution* was substituted, as the watchword of alarm. The Republicans were caricatured as mortal enemies to that sacred instrument, and determined, if their ticket should prevail, to prostrate it. When the public ear would no longer listen to that tale of slander, the people were assured with great horror, that their *Property* would be endangered by the success of the Republicans who were represented as bankrupts themselves, and combined to introduce a leveling system of laws, although they in fact possess three quarters of the solid property in the state. These successive misrepresentations, being refuted by experience, and having ceased to be believed, it has become necessary, in pursuance of the same system, to resort to some new pretext; and the *Embargo* is determined upon as the electioneering alarmbell for this year. An appeal is made, not to the reason, but to the passions and prejudices of the people. By means of letters, and speeches, and pamphlets, and committees, and missionaries, the State is filled with all manner of misrepresentations of that necessary measure. . . .

84 REPUBLICANS ATTEMPT TO TRANSFER JEFFERSON'S POPULARITY TO MADISON

Providence *Columbian Phenix,* June 18, 1808.

What is the reason why all *the British agents, emissaries, tories, refugees,* and all those who are opposed to the administration of Mr. Jefferson, are opposed to the election of Mr. MADISON to the Presidency? Because they know that he is the private and political friend of Mr. Jefferson—one who has had a principal share in the councils of his administration—one who is determined to oppose a submission to British taxation, and impressment of our seamen—and one who will defend the constitution he assisted in making against the wild attacks of a *Hillhouse,* etc. He will pursue the system of policy which has been practised by Mr. Jefferson—he will by all honorable means endeavor to preserve peace with all nations—practise economy—reduce the burthens of the country—carry into effect the extensive plan of internal improvement, which the government has conceived, and which is developed in Mr. Gallatin's late report. All the blessings which the country has enjoyed under the administration of Mr. Jefferson will be perpetuated. Mr. Madison has reached that age when the judgment is mature—and he has the advantage of great experience in public affairs. The friends of the present administration will support him upon the same ground as they would have supported Mr. Jefferson—and none but those who would have opposed Mr. Jefferson, had he again become a candidate, will oppose Mr. Madison. . . .

IX JEFFERSONIAN PATRONAGE

The victory of the Jeffersonian Republicans in the election of 1800 raised the question of the relationship of parties to patronage as it had never been posed before. The transfer of political control from the Federalists to the Republicans in 1801 marked the first party change-over in the national government, and the most pressing problem which the new administration had to face was what policy should be adopted in regard to Federalist office-holders. When John Adams had succeeded Washington as President in 1797, he had retained Washington's Cabinet as well as lesser officials and government workers. Adams never adopted a rigid policy of appointing only Federalists to office, but preference clearly was given to Federalists, and before his term of office expired Adams made every effort to fill all vacancies with Federalists. Included in his "midnight appointments" were a number of new judgeships and court officials created by the judiciary act passed by a Federalist-controlled Congress in February, 1801, only a few days before Adams's term ended on March 4. Federalists had also been given preference in the expansion of the army following the French war scare of 1798. On taking power, Republicans thus found federal offices, both civil and military, filled with Federalists, and many Republicans were demanding a clean sweep of Federalists from office. In attempting to work out a patronage policy, Jefferson devoted an inordinate amount of time to making appointments and removals, only to have his practices criticized by some as too moderate and condemned by others as too sweeping. The selections in this chapter trace the formation of patronage policy under Jefferson and the pressures within and without his party. They also clearly demonstrate that by Jefferson's time parties and patronage had become inseparably linked in American politics.

85 PRESIDENT JEFFERSON CONTEMPLATES POLICY

Jefferson found administering federal patronage one of the most burdensome duties of his office. He was working out guidelines to be followed as he wrote this letter, March 29, 1801, to Connecticut's Gideon Granger, who was to become Postmaster General in his administration. Many of his other letters written soon after his inauguration also protested against Adams's "midnight appointments." Ford, ed., *Writings of Thomas Jefferson*, VIII, 44-45.

. . . Nothing presents such difficulties of administration as offices. About appointments to them the rule is simple enough. The federalists having been in exclusive possession of them from the first origin of the party among us, to the 3d of Mar. 9 o'clock p.m. of the evening, at 12 of which Mr. A[dams] was to go out of office, their reason will acknowledge the justice of giving vacancies as they happen to those who have been so long excluded, till the same general proportion prevails in office which exist out of it. But removals are more difficult. No one will say that all should be removed, or that none should. Yet no two scarcely draw the same lines. I consider as nullities all the appointments (of a removable character) crowded in by Mr. Adams when he knew he was appointing counsellors and agents for his successor and not for himself. Persons who have perverted their offices to the oppression of their fellow citizens, as marshals packing juries, attorneys grinding their legal victims, intolerants removing those under them for opinion's sake, substitutes for honest men removed for their republican principles, will probably find few advocates even among their quondam party. But the freedom of opinion, and the reasonable maintenance of it, is not a crime, and ought not to occasion injury. These are as yet matters under consideration, our administration having never yet been assembled to decide finally on them. However some of them have in the meantime been acted on in cases which pressed. There is one in your state which calls for decision, and on which Judge [Levi] Lincoln will ask yourself and some others to consult and advise us. It is the case of Mr. Goodrich, whose being a recent appointment, made a few days only before Mr. Adams went out of office, is liable to the general nullification I affix to them. Yet there might be reason for continuing him: or if that would do more harm than good, we should inquire who is the person in the state who, superseding Mr. Goodrich, would from his character and standing in society, most effectually silence clamor, and justify the executive in a comparison of the two characters. For though I consider Mr. G[oodrich]'s appointment as a nullity in effect, yet others may view it as a possession and removal, and ask if that removal has been made to put in a better man? I pray you to take a broad view of this subject, consider it in all its bearings, local and general, and communicate to me your opinion. . . .

86 CONNECTICUT REPUBLICAN LEADERS EXPLAIN THEIR VIEWS ON PATRONAGE

President Jefferson soon came under heavy pressures to remove Federalists from office. Twenty-four prominent Connecticut Republicans, headed by Pierpont Edwards, signed this letter, June 4, 1801, to Attorney General Levi Lincoln, who passed it on to the President. Jefferson Papers, Library of Congress.

We are much obliged by the Candor and intelligence of your Communications . . . and will not hesitate to say that the peculiar state of politics in Connecticut has prevented our perception of the policy of Mr. Jefferson in delaying the removals from office, a Measure which appears to us absolutely necessary to the progress of republicanism here. We are aware that his position commands "a view of the whole ground" and that your situation has enabled you to regard the subject without prejudice and under advantages, which we have not enjoyed, and that in the general government, general rules must be adopted.

The reasons suggested by you for the present unfinished state of things are of unquestionable weight—the subject involves much interest and passion—republicans are not unanimous as to the extent and proper season of removals, and some whom we ought highly to respect, are for a general system of Conciliation without removals. But, Sir, even if it should be judged good policy in all other States, to retain the federalists in office, yet in this State, we could contemplate, in such policy only the certain ruin of republicanism and even by delays we apprehend a relapse, from which it will be difficult, perhaps impossible to recover. . . .

The season has now arrived, when it is necessary for us to organize, and to adopt measures for Conveying to our people just sentiments respecting the motives Measures and objects of the present administration and to obviate the false impressions which the federalists and federal papers have made and are making upon their minds. This organization will consist of a General Committee, of County Committees and of Subcommittees in the Towns of the State, and must be conducted with great fortitude and perseverance, through much labor and expense, to an end difficult to be attained but highly important to a republican administration. We expected that at this time federalism would have been humbled, and that our cause would advance under the most favorable auspices;—but [the] present session of assembly has shown us that a change in the presidency is not [to] change their system of persecution and abuse of which you have often heard, but which no man can fully realize unless he has seen and felt its effects. . . . Instead of bending before the General Will they set themselves up to be courted by the administration and feel at Liberty to practice on it every kind of caprice. We have the fullest confidence in the President: we accredit his zeal for our cause, his approbation of our exertions and we know that could he realize the embarrassments of republicanism in this State he would renounce the Idea of Conciliation in respect to our federal leaders. This being done our organization might proceed cheerfully and with fair prospects of success. . . .

. . . Considering the facts in our own State as a basis and perhaps somewhat under the influence of irritation we have judged, that a very extended system of removals would aid our cause—that republicanism was established at the Southward, and had so far advanced in New England that nothing was wanting but presidential patronage to Compleat it—that it was more important to retain the confidence of the majority than to Conciliate apparently men who can never be republicans. We have known that our Legislature could not be committed by any official expressions of political opinions and have therefore judged that other legislatures could not be pledged. And that republicanism must triumph rather by its own energies than by any balancing of contending parties—and that all the power of the Government thrown into the republican scale at this time would give it a decided and desirable preponderance. In fact we have been, and continue to be opposed to any conciliatory System from a persuasion that it cannot succeed and that a continuance of attempts to compose this object will throw us into imminent hazard:—But we are aware that all these conceptions may arise from the narrowness of our views and our local situation and that we may have erred in respect to the general policy. Those who have viewed this subject on a more extensive scale, can judge better than we can, yet we are persuaded that this state forms an exception to any conciliatory system.

The operating republicans here are few: they need every aid in advancing the cause—the Federal leaders are numerous, they have the influence of the Clergy, of federal papers, State offices and federal officers. Without the aid of these last, the republicans cannot encounter the others. The men whom we have to address, must be persuaded, not only that what we have before told them is true, but that our future communications to them may be relied on. These men do not discriminate accurately, they believe that merit and power are united, and they will listen especially on political subjects to men who enjoy the official confidence of administration. The republicans here expect that the President will remove the federalists from office nor is the expectation confined to candidates for office, it is general as far as we can judge. They are all mortified to see their enemies triumphing in a day when they expected triumph and to be daily insulted and abused as not having merited the confidence of the administration, whose advocates they have been. They are naturally ambitious that the confidence of the President should be openly extended to their friends and that he should repel from himself the unmerited reproach of indecision and timidity. But republicans are not the only Subjects of impression, there is a great number of men here, who always were and will be on the Strongest side. They have been federal, they are ready to be republican. There we should gain, if the removals were made. If the decided language of administration is to be that republicanism will prevail and that it is out of danger, these men will yield their confidence and aid to it; but if after all it should be decided to secure a semblance of affection from real enemies and to gain this point by leaving in their hands the weight of government, the cause of Mr. Jefferson and republicanism here is completely lost.

The proposed removals would bring the federalists into action, we will not Conceal it. They would denounce the measure as the result of a vindictive spirit, as the act of the President of a party, but this they have already said in respect to the removals made in other States. We conceive it better to meet them with all their force now, than three years hence, and we know, that they who seek occasion, will always find occasion for blame against any administration, and that their leaders will be opposed to Mr. Jeffersons reelection at any rate. . . . We cannot conceive, Sir, that our cause is to yield any sacrifices to any false constructions of Mr. Jeffersons Speech nor can we place a moments confidence in our cause, if it depends in the least on the conversion or acquiescence of a single federal leader. We are sure of a wise and faithful administration, and that a knowledge of its measures faithfully conveyed to our people will gain their confidence, but in Connecticut we must maintain a constant warfare with those men who have pledged themselves on a perpetual hostility to our cause. These remarks we make in the name of the general Committee of republicans here. . . . We do not wish the removals have to be made to an extent or at a season which will [be] prejudicial to the arrangements of any other State, and we believe that removals to the extent first proposed by us made at the present time, would not be to their prejudice but of this as of every other part of this letter, you will maturely judge and we confidently trust that the result will be for the good of the cause even though it may not accord with our feelings and these expressions of our opinions.

87 JEFFERSON ANNOUNCES HIS PATRONAGE POLICY

The removal of Federalist Elizur Goodrich and the appointment of Republican Samuel Bishop as collector of New Haven led a committee of the merchants of New Haven to send to the President a strongly worded remonstrance, to which Jefferson replied July 12, 1801. This reply, which was widely published in the press, was the most important public statement on patronage policy made by Jefferson during his presidency. Ford, ed., *Writings of Thomas Jefferson*, VIII, 67-70.

I have received the remonstrance you were pleased to address to me, on the appointment of Samuel Bishop to the office of collector of New Haven, lately vacated by the death of David Austin. The right of our fellow citizens to represent to the public functionaries their opinion on proceedings interesting to them, is unquestionably a constitutional right, often useful, sometimes necessary, and will always be respectfully acknowledged by me.

Of the various executive duties, no one excites more anxious concern than that of placing the interests of our fellow citizens in the hands of honest men, with understandings sufficient for their station. No duty, at the same time, is more difficult to fulfil. The knowledge of characters possessed by a single individual is, of necessity, limited. To seek out the best through the whole Union, we must resort to other information, which, from the best of men, acting disinterestedly and with the purest motives, is sometimes incorrect. In the case of Samuel Bishop, however, the subject of your remonstrance, time was taken, information was sought, and such obtained as could leave no room for doubt of his fitness. . . .

The removal, as it is called of Mr. Goodrich, forms another subject of complaint. Declarations by myself in favor of *political tolerance,* exhortations to *harmony* and affection in social intercourse, and to respect for the *equal rights* of the minority, have, on certain occasions, been quoted and misconstrued into assurances that the tenure of offices was to be undisturbed. But could candor apply such a construction? It is not indeed in the remonstrance that we find it; but it leads to the explanations which that calls for. When it is considered, that during the late administration, those who were not of a particular sect of politics were excluded from all office;

when, by a steady pursuit of this measure, nearly the whole offices of the U. S. were monopolized by that sect, when the public sentiment at length declared itself, and burst open the doors of honor and confidence to those whose opinions they more approved, was it to be imagined that this monopoly of office was still to be continued in the hands of the minority? Does it violate their *equal rights,* to assert some rights in the majority also? Is it *political intolerance* to claim a proportionate share in the direction of the public affairs? Can they not *harmonize* in society unless they have everything in their own hands? If the will of the nation, manifested by their various elections, calls for an administration of government according with the opinions of those elected; if, for the fulfilment of that will, displacements are necessary, with whom can they so justly begin as with persons appointed in the last moments of an administration, not for its own aid, but to begin a career at the same time with their successors, by whom they had never been approved, and who could scarcely expect from them a cordial co-operation? Mr. Goodrich was one of these. Was it proper for him to place himself in office, without knowing whether those whose agent he was to be would have confidence in his agency? Can the preference of another, as the successor to Mr. Austin, be candidly called a removal of Mr. Goodrich? If a due participation of office is a matter of right, how are vacancies to be obtained? Those by death are few; by resignation, none. Can any other mode than that of removal be proposed? This is a painful office; but it is made my duty, and I meet it as such. I proceed in the operation with deliberation and inquiry, that it may injure the best men least, and effect the purposes of justice and public utility with the least private distress; that it may be thrown, as much as possible, on delinquency, on oppression, on intolerance, on incompetence, on ante-revolutionary adherence to our enemies.

The remonstrance laments "that a change in the administration must produce a change in the subordinate officers;" in other words, that it should be deemed necessary for all officers to think with their principal. But on whom does this imputation bear? On those who have excluded from office every shade of opinion which was not theirs? Or on those who have been so excluded? I lament sincerely that unessential differences of political opinion should ever have been deemed sufficient to interdict half the society from the rights and the blessings of self-government, to proscribe them as characters unworthy of every trust. It would have been to me a circumstance of great relief, had I found a moderate participation of office in the hands of the majority. I would gladly have left to time and accident to raise them to their just share. But their total exclusion calls for prompter correctives. I shall correct the procedure; but that done, disdain to follow it,

shall return with joy to that state of things, when the only questions concerning a candidate shall be, is he honest? Is he capable? Is he faithful to
the Constitution?

88 THE REPUBLICAN PRESS RECALLS FEDERALIST POLICY

Boston *Independent Chronicle,* June 25, 1801.

Great complaints are made by the *Tory-Federalists,* that President
Jefferson has removed certain persons from office. Provided, however, he
had exercised this power to the utmost latitude, yet he could be justified by
the doings of the last administration. Were not Officers displaced for no
other cause than their political principles? Was not Mr. Adams justified in
all those papers, which now condemn President Jefferson? Was it not
urged that the men who were unfriendly to his administration ought not to
receive the bounties of government? Was it not established as a political
creed, that *confidence* in public officers, was the security by which the
harmony of the community was preserved? If these things were admitted
under Mr. Adams, why do they not equally apply to Mr. Jefferson? . . .

89 REPUBLICAN NEWSPAPERS CALL FOR EXTENSIVE REMOVALS

New York *American Citizen,* June 5, 1801.

Hitherto the removal of Tories from office, and the appointment of
Republicans in lieu of them, has been, we confess, so solitary and unfre-
quent, that the Republicans have as great complaints to make in this respect,
as the Tories have for any removal at all of people of their own sentiments.
It was ardently desired and confidently expected by the Republicans of New-
York, (for of them only can we directly speak) that by this time *one half at
least* of the Tories *now in office* in the United States, would have been
removed; and its not being done has occasioned, we solemnly and reluc-
tantly confess, very serious apprehensions and doubts in the public mind,
which are every day increasing.—Nor have we reason to believe it is otherwise throughout the United States. It is rational to suppose that those who
removed John Adams from office, because of his manifold transgressions
of the constitution, and his pointed hostility to liberty—those by whose
exertions a standing army was disbanded—alien and sedition laws de-

stroyed—four millions of dollars, the proceeds of oppressive taxes, cut off—That those who had occasioned the removal of the capital offenders against the state, and restored the shattered constitution to its primitive condition, would naturally expect the removal of the lesser culprits in office. If this should not be the case, for what, in the name of God, have we been contending? Merely for the removal of John Adams, that Mr. Jefferson might occupy the place which he shamefully left? It cannot be! Those who view the Republicans in this light are egregiously mistaken, and will find themselves disappointed in their erroneous calculations.

Four years of an administration, all things considered, the most expensive, the most wicked, the most turbulent, and the most destructive of national liberty and happiness ever witnessed in modern times, have convinced our republican citizens that, while a man remains in office who contributed to this state of things, to which we cannot look back but with horror, neither the constitution can be safe, nor themselves satisfied. Of this the evident sense of the country cannot be misunderstood. It has been expressed in language plain, energetic, and decisive. And an administration less plain, less energetic, and less decisive, *will not* satisfy the country. *Temporising policy,* under all the present circumstances of the United States, to say the least, will render unpopular, if not odious, an administration to which the republicans, for four years back, have been looking up as the summit of their hopes, and the conservator of their liberty. Nor will they, we are confident, be deceived. Mr. Jefferson's attachment to the constitution, and his fine sense of the necessity of obeying the voice of the people, are pledges that his administration will answer all their expectations, and comport with their will.

Hartford *American Mercury,* July 30, 1801, reprinted from the Philadelphia *Aurora.*

I am bold to say, that the unequivocal wish of the people who have borne the obloquy, abuse, and deprivations, and who on account of their political opinions were treated as outcasts in society, during the reign of terror, is that *the board should be swept.*

So far from apologizing for Mr. Jefferson's removing from office, I say his not doing so requires the apology.—I say it is what the people expect, what both parties struggled for and expected to see;—it was as well understood previous to the elections, that men who had advocated the baleful measures of several years past, who have been persecutors of the friends of republicanism, were to be removed and the offices filled by men of republican principles, if they succeeded in their candidates, as if it had been reduced to a written contract.

It was no more doubted by men in office, that they would go out with Mr. Adams, than that Jefferson would succeed Adams; nay, they said so, they wrote so, they expected it, and acted accordingly; no trimming, no preparation to fall in with the strongest, but public exertion, declamation, and abuse, were more openly employed by the officers of government than by almost any other. Surely then it cannot be expected that such men can be trusted either upon terms of respect or policy; Mr. Jefferson does not mean to offend his friends, or to disappoint the people who elected him of their wishes, and deprive them of their right, namely, to have the offices filled with men whose conduct and sentiments are congenial with the Constitution, and consistent with a pacific and economical administration. It was in confidence that he would cure these evils he was elected, not to reconcile parties who are found irreconcileable; no, they are not to be conciliated, neither should their conciliation be purchased at so great a price, as the total disregard of the wishes of the genuine republicans, the majority of the people—for offended they must be, if Mr. Jefferson should continue in office, the persons who menaced them with death, treated them with insult. insolence, and contempt, merely for adhering to the principles of '76, expressing their approbation of his character and sentiments—How many men are persecuted with lawsuits, proscribed in their business, and ruined in their reputation merely for continuing firm to republicanism, and opposing the outrageous and shameless measures of Mr. Adams and his creatures? Could men who thus suffered, be treated more cruelly by Mr. Jefferson, than to continue the same officers, the same oppressors and persecutors, the same creatures of corruption in office over them! To continue arms in the hands of their enemies, even after they have been vanquished, has never been a general policy, there may be some men of honor and moderation, in office who may be trusted, but certain it is, that to continue persecutors in office, is to keep arms in the hands of inveterate enemies, who would daily use them to our destruction.

Neither is there any view of the subject which does not shew the necessity of removals—*Rotation in office,* is the essence of Republicanism by keeping the people more on a level, disposing them to pursuits of industry, instead of making a trade of the public services—diffusing a knowledge of office more generally among the citizens—producing final settlements—discovering frauds and counteracting favoritism—the propriety of having a republican government administered by republicans rather than by monarchists, by the friends of America rather than the friends of any foreign country, and in fact the keeping awake and in action the power and energy of so many minds leads to improvement in system, fidelity in practice, general habits of vigilance among the people—with so many political advantages to society —with so strong a claim of justice to individuals, and with this plain and evident proposition, that all who contribute to the support of government, and are qualified, ought to share in the benefits thereof in common—The cause for dismissal is sufficient that they have had their share; we say, and declare it aloud as the unanimous voice of Republicanism, that the least to be expected from Mr. Jefferson, is the removal from office of every man who has been a persecutor, a supporter of extravagant and wicked measures.

90 FEDERALISTS PROTEST REPUBLICAN REMOVALS

While a large segment of the Republican party regarded Jefferson's policy as too moderate, Federalists generally condemned the President for lack of moderation, as the following remarks by two leading Federalists indicate. Henry M. Wagstaff, ed., *The Papers of John Steele* (Raleigh: 1924), I, 260-61; Baldwin Family Papers, Yale University.

Oliver Wolcott to John Steele
March 12, 1802

The freedom of our Elections, has been virtually destroyed, by the conduct of the President in making new appointments—he has incited a spirit of rivalship, passion and resentment, which is utterly uncontrolable. Every four years, while the present government lasts we shall be called to elect a President and with him a compleat sett of executive officers, down to the most subordinate grades. The passions which will be incited by rival Candidates, will soon render peaceable Elections impracticable.

Simeon Baldwin to Jared Mansfield
January 16, 1804

I do consider the wanton abuse of the necessary power of removal, as one of the darkest traits in the character of our present chief magistrate. That those who are the constitutional advisers of the executive should be of the same political sentiments with him I readily admit, for a change in such officers, I never blame him—but I cannot forgive him for removing a host of inferior officers who were *honest, faithful* and *capable,* and whose political sentiments had no connexion with the discharge of their official Duties.

It was an extension of the arm of power, that I believe no prime minister, or even monarch in Europe ever dared to use.

91 THE SECRETARY OF WAR OUTLINES POLICY ON ARMY APPOINTMENTS

Jefferson's Secretary of War, Henry Dearborn, made it clear that in appointments to the army, Republicans were to be preferred. Henry Dearborn Papers and William Eustis Papers, Library of Congress.

To William Eustis
  May 2, 1808

Your letter in favor of Mr. Clark has been received. I wish you had added what his political standing is. We have at present a sufficient proportion of our political opponents in the Army, to render any new appointments, in the small body of additional troops, of that class, unnecessary, if not inexpedient,—and after the outragious conduct of that party within the last few months, no individual among them can pretend to any claim on the Government. If giving a Commission, is to be considered a favour conferred on the individual who receives it, ought such favours to be granted to men who have constantly mustered in the ranks of our outragious bitter and inveterate enemies, and especially at the present moment, after a full display of their violent hostility. A young Gentleman by the name of James Grafton, from Boston, has lately arrived here for a commission. . . . Another by the name of Samuel Miller who has lived in Boston, in Taunton and elsewhere, has been here all winter waiting for an appointment. . . . I will thank you to be so obliging as to ascertain their political charactors and let me know what you can learn relative to them, and also what is the political standing of Mr. Clark, mentioned in your last letter. . . . As far as I am informed, I presume that about two thirds of the candidates recommended from Massachusetts, are federalists. If I recommend any such to the President, it will be from the effect of deception. If we were to have a serious War, and of course have a large Army, I should think it proper to give all classes of society an opportunity of defending the Country, who should be so disposed, but I should, even in that case, doubt the propriety of confiding any considerable command to Essex Junto men, or any other Monarchical Gentlemen.

To Joseph B. Varnum
June 12, 1808

Your favor of the 31st ultimo has been received. I accord fully with you in sentiment, in relation to the expediency of caution in giving any appointments to such as may not be disposed to defend the best interests of our Country. I had noticed with some surprise, the undue proportion of federalists recommended for commissions from Massachusetts, and it has been a subject of deep regret, to find a large proportion of such charactors recommended by our best friends, or by those who rank high in the republican Causes. You have not yet recommended a charactor for Captain of Cavalry;—I am very glad that Colonel Boyd has satisfied you that he is correct in his politics, I had some doubts. . . . From the specimens already discovered, I conclude the Federalist party in Massachusetts, will, while in power, afford a strong example of what our conduct towards them ought to be, in relation to offices and appointments. We have been much more liberal towards them, than they would be towards us, and in future I think we ought to give them measure for measure.

Epilogue

Together with many of their contemporaries long since forgotten, the men whose words have filled these pages were responsible for the making of the American party system. Although they may not have understood what they were building, they contributed to the workability of the American system of self-government in which political parties became an important part of the process of translating popular aspirations into governmental policy. Many of the techniques of parties developed in the early Republic have survived the test of time. It is indeed instructive to observe that so many of the statesmen of the young nation were skillful political practitioners. Surely an important element of the heritage from the early American Republic is an aptitude, if not always an affinity, for practical politics.

The Eyewitness Accounts of American History Series